A Patterned Life

A Patterned Life

Faith, History, and David Bebbington

EILEEN BEBBINGTON

FOREWORD BY
TIMOTHY LARSEN

WIPF & STOCK · Eugene, Oregon

A PATTERNED LIFE
Faith, History, and David Bebbington

Copyright © 2014 Eileen Bebbington. All rights reserved. Except for brief quotations in critical publications or reviews, no part of this book may be reproduced in any manner without prior written permission from the publisher. Write: Permissions. Wipf and Stock Publishers, 199 W. 8th Ave., Suite 3, Eugene, OR 97401.

Wipf and Stock
An Imprint of Wipf and Stock Publishers
199 W. 8th Ave., Suite 3
Eugene, OR 97401

www.wipfandstock.com

ISBN 13: 978-1-62564-929-4

Manufactured in the U.S.A.   10/20/2014

Contents

List of Illustrations | vi
Foreword by Timothy Larsen | vii
Preface | xv

Prologue | 1
1   The Nottingham Years | 3
2   The Cambridge Years | 35
3   The Stirling Years | 64
4   Conclusion | 105

Appendix 1: The Use of History | 107
Appendix 2: William Wilberforce and Christian Duty | 112
Appendix 3: The Christian Scholar and the Scriptures | 121
Appendix 4: Curriculum Vitae of David Bebbington | 131
Appendix 5: Books Published by David Bebbington | 133

Index | 135

List of Illustrations

1. David aged 9 months with his parents, Bill and Vera | 4
2. David aged 2 | 5
3. Alec Urquhart's shop, 11 Belvedere Street, Mansfield | 12
4. 31 Covedale Road, Sherwood, Nottingham | 14
5. Seely Primary School Assembly Hall | 16
6. Nottingham High School | 21
7. Queensberry Street Baptist Church, Old Basford, Nottingham | 25
8. David aged about 15 with his father on holiday | 31
9. Jesus College, Cambridge | 36
10. St. Andrew's Street Baptist Church, Cambridge | 41
11. David and Eileen's wedding, 1971 | 52
12. 1 New Square, Cambridge, seen from Christ's Pieces | 53
13. 69 Richmond Road, Cambridge | 55
14. Fitzwilliam College, Cambridge | 58
15. 5 Pullar Avenue, Bridge of Allan | 65
16. David aged 37, Anne aged 2, on holiday, South London | 67
17. David aged 56, Anne aged 21, in Waco, Texas | 70
18. University of Stirling | 72
19. David aged 29, author of *Patterns in History* | 74
20. Keiss Baptist Church, Sutherland, on its 250th anniversary | 77
21. The Calvin Quatercentenary Conference, Geneva, 2009 | 85
22. Family group in Waco, Texas, 2009 | 88
23. *Evangelicalism in Modern Britain*, 1989 | 92
24. David in secondhand bookshop, Eastbourne, Sussex, 1983 | 96
25. Eileen and David, Waco, Texas, 2011 | 100

Foreword

DAVID BEBBINGTON IS A highly honored historian—one thinks immediately of his personal professorial chair at the University of Stirling, his presidency of the Ecclesiastical History Society, his long association with Baylor University as a Visiting Distinguished Professor, the numerous endowed lecture series that he has been chosen to deliver, and much more. He is also a popular historian: his name is often evoked even by undergraduate students in a whole variety of countries and he is sought out by members of the media to comment on current news stories. (I remember being delighted during one of my doctoral tutorials when he took a call from a journalist from the popular tabloid the *Daily Mail*—a newspaper that sells something approaching two million papers daily!)

Nevertheless, Bebbington is not among the *most* popular of historians: his books do not end up on general nonfiction bestseller lists and he is not one of those celebrity academics who are seen hosting big-budget documentaries on television. He is also not, as of yet, one of the *most* honored historians: he is still a little young for the age when what are the most coveted prizes are bestowed on their extraordinarily favored recipients, and so we shall have to wait and see whether any of those materialize.

David Bebbington is, however, one of the most *influential* of historians. Indeed, scholars who are more popular and more honored are nonetheless manifestly less influential than him. Historians should generally resist the temptation to try to be prophets but, still—precisely because they are keen observers of change and continuity over time—they can sometimes see more clearly than others how things are likely to play out in the future. With that warrant, I confidently predict that Bebbington's scholarship will still be influencing people's thinking in significant ways long after all the impressions are gone of the majority of today's most popular and honored historians.

Foreword

But one only needs eyes and not the gift of prophecy to notice Bebbington's extraordinary influence over the last several decades and at this present time. The most obvious indicator of that influence is his famous definition of evangelicalism, widely referred to as the "Bebbington quadrilateral." How many other historians can you think of whose very name has been incorporated into the explanation of a major historical reality? The wider world was introduced to Bebbington's four distinguishing characteristics of evangelicalism—conversionism, activism, biblicism, and crucicentrism—in 1989 with the publication of his *Evangelicalism in Modern Britain*.[1] By that time, evangelicalism was already an established preoccupation of the American media and social commentators. Well over a decade earlier, *Newsweek* magazine had dubbed 1976 the "Year of the Evangelical." This fixation only increased in the 1980s when pollsters and pundits decided that evangelicals were a decisive voting block that could determine the outcome of national elections. Moreover, as its title proclaimed, Bebbington's book was about religion in Britain. It is thus truly astonishing that he analyzed such a widely discussed movement and ended up providing *the* standard definition of it—not only for Britain, but also for America, and indeed for the entire world, with global evangelicalism emerging as a major force in Africa, Latin America, and Asia in the twenty-first century.

It is difficult to overstate the near monopoly position that the Bebbington Quadrilateral has on defining evangelicalism.[2] Of course, other scholars have put forward other definitions since 1989, but they have made virtually no impact at all: everyone just continues evoking the four marks expounded by the professor from Stirling. This is all the more remarkable when one considers that this Christian movement had already existed for some 250 years before *Evangelicalism in Modern Britain*. The transatlantic world was crowded with churches, denominations, charities, and parachurch organizations that self-identified as "evangelical;" some had already done so decades before the United States of America had even been founded. How could a definition not have been settled on before 1989? Indeed, often these very venerable evangelical organizations now deploy the Bebbington Quadrilateral to explain what they have meant all along by "evangelical"—a term they were using as a self-descriptor long before Beb-

---

1. *Evangelicalism in Modern Britain: A History from the 1730s to the 1980s* (London: Unwin Hyman, 1989).

2. For documentation of this claim, see Larsen, "The Reception Given *Evangelicalism in Modern Britain* since Its Publication in 1989," in Haykin and Stewart (eds.), *The Advent of Evangelicalism: Exploring Historical Continuities* (Nashville: B&H Academic, 2008).

FOREWORD

bington was born! Bebbington's definition of evangelicalism is the standard one in both secular contexts and Christian ones and for journalists and other popularizers as well as academics and other specialists.

Once one moves beyond this paramount achievement, Bebbington's greatest impact has undoubtedly been on the Christian community, especially among Christian scholars. Nevertheless, it is worth highlighting briefly some of Bebbington's other influences on secular scholars before moving on to this second major theme. This will be addressed more directly below, but one factor has been enabling scholars to appreciate the nature and depth of religious convictions as a shaping force in history generally, including intellectual, political, and cultural history. Admirers of the work of David Bebbington in America and around the world are often completely unaware that back in Britain he is also recognized as a noted political historian. The book that emerged from his PhD research, *The Nonconformist Conscience: Chapel and Politics, 1870–1914*, although it was published over thirty years ago now, still holds a strong place on the reading lists of many courses at secular universities in Britain.[3] It is widely recognized for lucidly and convincingly explaining a powerful force in British politics in the nineteenth and early twentieth centuries. Bebbington's *magnum opus* in terms of political history, however, is *The Mind of Gladstone: Religion, Homer, and Politics* (2004).[4] As the only prime minister to serve four terms, William E. Gladstone occupies a British position equivalent to the prominent place that Franklin D. Roosevelt holds in American politics. No one has ever gone deeper into the influences that shaped Gladstone's thinking, and thus all scholars who want to understand who Gladstone was rather than merely what he did must henceforth consult Bebbington's seminal volume. An indirect influence is the army of PhD students that David Bebbington has supervised. The recent appointment of his former doctoral student, Jonathan Yeager, to a tenure-track position at the University of Tennessee at Chattanooga is just one example of Bebbington's influence spreading out into the secular academy. Moreover, innumerable secular scholars read and are significantly shaped by both Bebbington's own publications and those of scholars who were trained under his supervision.

Beside his definition of evangelicalism, however, Bebbington's greatest influence has undoubtedly been in Christian circles, especially scholarly ones. This began with another dramatic splash: the publication in 1979

---

3. London: Allen & Unwin, 1982.
4. Oxford: Oxford University Press, 2004.

of *Patterns in History*.[5] Once again, Bebbington somehow got there first. In America, there was a growing conversation in Christian higher education about the need to integrate faith and learning. One key catalyst for this a few years earlier had been Arthur Holmes's *The Idea of a Christian College* (1975).[6] This programmatic call necessitated disciplinary-specific responses. Historiography had to rely on Herbert Butterfield's *Christianity and History* (1949), a book written in a quite different period both in terms of what were the dominant intellectual challenges and in terms of the level of acceptance of Christian thought in the wider academy.[7] (One illustration of this much more established position for Christianity in the 1940s is the fact that *Christianity and History* was originally a series of lectures broadcast on the BBC's Third Programme, a premier cultural and intellectual venue for the British nation as a whole.) The Conference on Faith and History had already been founded in 1967, and there were hundreds of Christian colleges and universities where history professors longed to have a substantial, up-to-date account of the difference that their faith might make to their approach to their discipline. As there was not anything like as large or well-organized a group of Christian academics in Britain, it is all the more surprising that a British scholar was the one to meet this need. Nevertheless, *Patterns in History* quickly became the standard book to assign or recommend for anyone interested in the integration of faith and the discipline of history. From this triumphant start, Bebbington has gone on from strength to strength over the decades until he is now universally esteemed as a senior statesman for a Christian approach to history.[8]

Indeed, history became one of the disciplines in which evangelical scholars emerged as most influential and successful in the last third of the twentieth century. In an American context in the 1980s this achievement

---

5. Downers Grove: InterVarsity, 1979.

6. Grand Rapids: Eerdmans, 1975. Chapter 4 was entitled, "Integrating Faith and Learning."

7. London: Bell, 1949.

8. To give just a few random examples, he was invited to give the magisterial summation to a volume with such leading contributors as Mark A. Noll, John Coffey, and Brad S. Gregory (Bebbington, "The History of Ideas and the Study of Religion," in Chapman, Coffey, and Gregory, *Seeing Things Their Way: Intellectual History and the Return of Religion* [Notre Dame: University of Notre Dame Press, 2009]), and he was asked to represent history in a volume that covered a wide variety of academic disciplines: Bebbington, "The Discipline of History and the Perspective of Faith since 1900," in Lundin, *Christ across the Disciplines: Past, Present, Future* (Grand Rapids: Eerdmans, 2013).

Foreword

was identified as "the New Evangelical Historiography."[9] Its father figure was George Marsden and its self-sacrificial, energetic, network builder was Mark Noll. By 1996, an entire book had already been written on the work of these evangelical historians.[10] This was a cohort in America—a band of brothers and sisters—and these scholars were overwhelmingly on the faculties of Christian colleges and universities. George Rawlyk, however, was in a class of his own in this network in Canada—as was David Bebbington in Britain. This made it all the more strategic that Bebbington was the evangelical historian pursuing the task of the integration of faith and learning who would be the one to rise to the rank of full professor in the History Department of a secular, British university. (Others have followed in this path that Bebbington blazed: one thinks, in particular, of John Coffey at the University of Leicester.) Part of the reason why Bebbington has supervised so many American PhD students is because the leading evangelical historians in the United States often did not teach at institutions that had doctoral programs in history. Ironically, it proved to be more valuable and strategic even for the evangelical movement in the United States for Professor Bebbington to be at the University of Stirling rather than on the faculty of an American institution.

The last area of influence I will highlight here is the connection between religious history and intellectual history. Bebbington has made significant contributions not only as a religious historian and as a political historian, but also as an intellectual historian. This was the real, substantive achievement of *Evangelicalism in Modern Britain*, which presented the Bebbington Quadrilateral merely as a bit of preliminary ground clearing for the main task of uncovering the connections between the history of evangelicalism and the great intellectual movements of the Enlightenment, Romanticism, and Modernism. Hitherto evangelicalism had often been viewed—even by evangelical scholars—as a kind of intellectual backwater that was largely cut off from the main intellectual currents of society and which was usually hostile and obstructionist when it did encounter them. Evangelicalism was the gigantic, obscurantist Party of No: the Enlightenment was too rationalistic, Modernism was too relativistic, and Romanticism was, well, too romantic. Bebbington demonstrated that the evangelical movement was not

---

9. Sweet, "Wise as Serpents, Innocent as Doves: The New Evangelical Historiography," *Journal of the American Academy of Religion*, 56 (1988) 397–416.

10. Burch, *The Evangelical Historians: The Historiography of George Marsden, Nathan Hatch, and Mark Noll* (Lanham: University Press of America, 1996).

only much more in touch with the main ideas of the times than had been assumed, but also impressively skilled at imbibing them and making use of them for its own ends. These views are widely assumed today—whole books are written premised on them—but Bebbington is the font from which they flow.[11] A major contribution along these lines is a recent, formidable, masterly work by David Bebbington, *Victorian Religious Revivals: Culture and Piety in Local and Global Contexts* (2012).[12] The history of religious revivals had been a dubious, if not discredited, field which was seen as embarrassingly old-fashioned and fatally tainted with pious legends, wishful thinking, rigged providentialism, and polemical special pleading. Bebbington brilliantly set it back on its academic footing as an up-to-date, credible, scholarly field of inquiry. Along the way, he also showed that these people who have been stereotyped as ignorant fanatics, were often well read, sophisticated, and intellectually current. *Victorian Religious Revivals* is also a splendid example of Bebbington's macro/micro approach to history, connecting charming, meticulously researched local case studies with the grand themes sweeping across the continents and the centuries.

I think I have said enough now to enable readers to grasp Bebbington's extraordinary influence. I have not been asked to introduce the book itself, but I will take the liberty to offer a little bit of a transition to the main contents of *A Patterned Life: Faith, History, and David Bebbington* by way of a kind of coda. Eileen Bebbington has written a study that is both valuable and enjoyable. It is a fascinating and entertaining read because of her delightful candor and her exquisite eye for the telling detail and anecdote. The humor usually arises from the comedy inherit in the human condition, though occasionally she helps it along. (I particularly relished her aside after recounting an ill-judged early sermon that Bebbington preached: "Fortunately that chapel is still open . . .") For those of us who know David Bebbington personally, of course, many things fall into place after reading this account of his life. To take a trivial example, everyone who knows him at all knows of his monumentally vast personal library and of his obsession with collecting books. He once told me that he had been searching for certain coveted volumes for decades now. This was not long after secondhand bookshops from around the world started putting their stock lists all in one

---

11. To take two obvious examples to hand, Yeager, *Enlightened Evangelicalism: The Life and Thought of John Erskine* (New York: Oxford University Press, 2011); Hopkins, *Nonconformity's Romantic Generation: Evangelical and Liberal Theologies in Victorian England* (Milton Keynes: Paternoster, 2004).

12. Oxford: Oxford University Press, 2012.

Foreword

place on searchable websites and I was therefore thrilled with the possibility of being able to be the agent for fulfilling some of these long-standing ambitions. To my surprise, however, Bebbington resolutely refused these offers. Observing this hobby arise from an earlier one of spotting bus numbers, I now better understand how this would have somehow felt like "cheating" to him! Then there is his love of mouthful words and his tendency to assume that others know more than they do. I remember fondly having a meal with my by then former PhD supervisor in a restaurant in America, the minimum-wage-earning server bringing the bill to our table, and Professor Bebbington looking this poor teenager in the eyes and asking brightly about his policy on "disaggregation"! More soberly, Bebbington has, at least in my experience, always masked just how debilitating his suffering from ME (Chronic Fatigue Syndrome) has been with minimizing assessments and determined cheerfulness. I still remember, however, visiting for a tutorial and going for lunch with him at the University of Stirling's cafeteria. This little trip across campus included one short flight of stairs. Professor Bebbington used all of the strength in both of his arms to help pull himself up them one excruciating step after the next. To read that he ended up sleeping downstairs because he could no longer make it to his own bedroom is to wonder in astonishment at both his productivity and his good humor.

For those who do not know him personally, however, this book is not only a lively read and an account of an important scholar, but it is also itself an evocative history of past times and places, documenting for the ages a Nonconformist chapel subculture that is now gone, Cambridge University life as it was for earnest young Christians in the late 1960s and the 1970s, and much more as Bebbington moves forward in time and back and forth across the globe. The University of Stirling should commission him to write its history as he has been on the scene for what is fast approaching four-fifths of its entire history! And many readers will be fascinated by Bebbington's encounters with other remarkable, well-known figures from the past and present. (I was particularly delighted by the youthful Bebbington's naïve hope that he could persuade Eamon Duffy to become a Protestant!) I shall resist the temptation to steal Mrs. Bebbington's thunder any further, however. Reader, read on!

—Timothy Larsen, May 2014
Wheaton College, Illinois

Preface

HISTORY IS AT THE heart of the Christian faith. Christians believe that Jesus Christ, a first-century Jew, was also God himself, and that subsequent human history has been profoundly affected by Jesus' birth, death, and resurrection. Many historians over the years have investigated how Christian faith and history are connected with each other. A modern example of such a historian is David Bebbington who, during his long career at the University of Stirling in Scotland, has explored how the relationship has worked out in practice at various levels. His book *Patterns in History*, for example, considers the ways in which large movements of thought in the past, including the Christian faith, have influenced how people have viewed the processes of history. He has also written several books about how evangelical Christianity spread first through Britain and America and then across the world. He is best known for his way of characterising evangelicalism, the so-called "Bebbington quadrilateral." This book is about what influences, Christian and historical as well as many others, affected his development as he grew up in the second half of the twentieth century in Britain, leading him to devote his career to this subject.

The most obvious person to write this memoir was David himself but, since he has a long queue of books still waiting to be written, an autobiography was not in prospect. As his wife, I therefore decided that I was the next best person as I had shared most of the last forty-six years with him and have seen his thought develop. The idea for this book first came into my mind when David started receiving questions from students in the United States who were working on his books. How did the "Bebbington quadrilateral" come into being? What has influenced his thinking over the years? How can a historian be interested in the Christian faith in a scientifically dominated twenty-first-century world? As I wrote, I realised that there were many points of interest. Some of the great movements of the

Preface

time had a direct impact on David's life: the First World War, the Second World War, and the economic depression between the two. He had educational opportunities that have vanished from today's Britain while higher education has expanded beyond all expectations. Above all it is a story of a person whose Christian faith and love of history have been intertwined for very nearly sixty years.

In order to expand certain points I have included three unpublished pieces of writing by David which form the first three appendices. The first is "The Use of History," which is the text of an address which has been given in various places and which includes some of the main reasons why David believes history is important. The second, "William Wilberforce and Christian Duty," provides an example of a sermon interwoven with history which is one of David's specialities. The third, "The Christian Scholar and the Scriptures," gives insight into what David feels about the responsibilities carried by Christian scholars, whatever their discipline. For ease of reference I have included a brief *curriculum vitae* and a list of David's books as appendices 4 and 5.

If anyone would like to read more on how David developed his thinking about history, it can be found in his essay "The Discipline of History and the Perspective of Faith since 1900," originally a lecture given at Wheaton College, Illinois, but then published in Roger Lundin (ed.), *Christ across the Disciplines: Past, Present, Future*.[1] The broad trends of the period in his main field are examined in a paper he gave to the Ecclesiastical History Society and published as "The Evangelical Discovery of History" in Peter D. Clarke and Charlotte Methuen (eds.), *The Church on Its Past*.[2] The present book is altogether more personal.

I am grateful to those who have encouraged me along the way: to Charlie Phillips and Tim Larsen, and to Anne, our daughter, who never wavered in her support for the project. I am especially grateful to Tim for writing the foreword. My deep thanks go to David for patiently answering my many, many questions about his past, often while we have been at Chinese restaurants at various times over the last three years. I thank him with great affection, too, for the constant interest and enrichment that he has brought to my life. And I am supremely grateful to God for arranging that David and I should have met at all in Cambridge in 1968 and for being with us ever since.

1. Grand Rapids: Eerdmans, 2013.
2. Woodbridge, Suffolk: Boydell, 2013.

Preface

I want to thank Matt Foley for bringing the manuscript into acceptable format, a task way beyond me, and David Cumming and Hugh McWhinnie for help with the photographs. That task is definitely beyond me too. Thank you to Wayne Boucher of Cambridge 2000 for his kindness over the photographs of Jesus College, Fitzwilliam College and St. Andrew's Street Baptist Church. I should add that, despite David's answers to my questions, this book is very much my own work rather than his. He read it to check for accuracy only at the final stage, and so the opinions are mine. I dedicate this book to our grandchildren, Becky and Daniel, with thanks for the laughter and fun they have brought into our lives, in the hope that in the future they will enjoy understanding more about their grandpa.

—Eileen Bebbington
Stirling, May 2014

Prologue

OVER NEW YEAR 2014, David attended a session of the American Society of Church History in Washington, DC. Although he is used to attending conference sessions, this occasion was different for him because its focus was the impact that one of his own books had made since its publication twenty-five years previously with special reference to the "Bebbington quadrilateral," a definition of evangelicalism that had come into widespread usage. He approached the time away with excitement—trips have always meant escape and freedom to him—and with his usual thorough planning. Armed with three guide books to read on the plane, off he flew. Once he had prioritized the sights he wanted to visit and refreshed himself on the history of the city, he was ready to begin. He met up with many old friends from across the United States with whom he had meals, including colleagues from Baylor University, Texas, where he had often worked. The idea for the session had been suggested by Charlie Phillips, one of his ex-PhD students who had become Senior Analyst and National Program Officer for the Maclellan Foundation, an American grant-giving trust, together with another ex-PhD student, Jonathan Yeager, now of the University of Tennessee, Chattanooga. Other former PhD students were there and one of his current students flew in for the day from Louisiana. Apart from the conference session itself, David managed to include most of his favorite activities: visits to the sights on his list, extensive walking to understand the geography and the buildings of the city, visits to as many secondhand bookshops / used bookstores as possible, gift shopping, and meals at Chinese restaurants. A highlight was the Sunday with two services at Capitol Hill Baptist Church where he spoke at length with their pastor with whom he had many contacts in common and who generously allowed him to take as many books as he liked from the church bookstall. How, then, had it come about that a small boy in the East Midlands of England with parents who had received little formal education had become this person visiting Washington? How had he written books that had become so well known? Where had the interests originated that filled his time in Washington? And how had it arisen that in the twelve months around that New Year he would visit North America five times including a four-month work period? This story could not happen in the same way now because the opportunities would not be open to a boy from his school. This adds interest to his story.

1

The Nottingham Years

FAMILY

Having been born on July 25, 1949, in a nursing home in the city of Nottingham in the East Midlands of England, David grew up with his parents in their own house, 31 Covedale Road, in Sherwood, one of the city's northern suburbs. His father, William (known as Bill), had spent much of his life in the city, but his mother, Vera, had grown up in Mansfield, a town then at the center of the coal mining community, some fourteen miles to the north. Bill had served in the army during the Second World War in the Far East. On his return in 1946 he wanted to be with his wife as much as possible after the long absence abroad and so he joined Vera and her father in their chiropody/podiatry business in Belvedere Street, Mansfield. Bill and Vera had hoped for a baby for some years. At thirty-six and thirty-three, respectively, they felt time was not on their side.

David aged 9 months with his parents, Bill and Vera

Vera loved her new baby when he came three years later, but she was an anxious mother, eager to "get it right" but without any real experience of babies to help her. She kept a strict routine and so David was born into a pattern. Indeed, David's bedtime was still 6 p.m. until he was nearly five years old! Vera stopped work in these early years and it must have been quite a lonely time for her without any antenatal classes or mother and baby groups. There was actually no public mention of pregnancy at all. She was mortified when, at seven months pregnant, a man at a wedding offered her a chair to sit on because it meant that he knew she was expecting a baby. Young mothers did not meet to share advice and so Vera was quite isolated. She did not have a warm relationship with her mother. Often Bill would leave well before eight in the morning to catch the bus to Mansfield and would not return until David was in bed. Most of the houses on Covedale Road had been built just before the Second World War and had then had young parents in them. Now their children were ten years older than David and not playmates for him. The one bright spot was Bill's sister, David's Auntie Madge, who lived in Nottingham with her husband, Norman, until David was two. She had three children of her own, Trevor, Margaret, and Alan, and helped to boost Vera's confidence. David stayed close to his auntie until her death in 2000.

The Nottingham Years

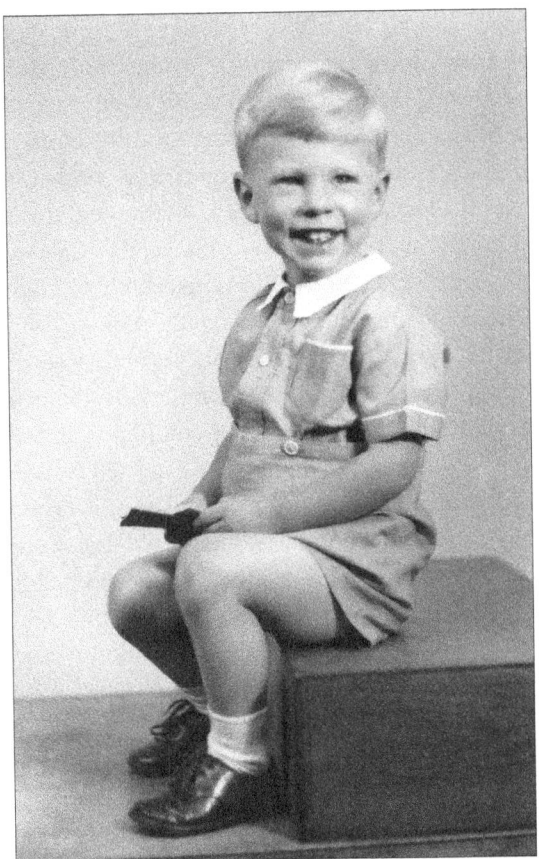

David aged 2

As soon as he could walk, David was expected to go quite long distances with his mother. Once, on a visit to a local shop at a distance of a mile away, up and down some steepish hills, Vera was irritated when a passerby suggested that it was a long walk for such a small boy as she felt that could be sowing seeds in his young mind that it could indeed be a long way! Pattern was strong in daily life. Until David was well into his teens, food was simple: breakfast consisted of bacon, bread, and milk, and lunch tended to be the same each week. For example, a sirloin of beef was roasted on Sundays with potatoes, peas, and, oddly, mint sauce (which the British usually eat with lamb), always followed by a very milky rice pudding (a Bebbington family tradition). On the other days of the week the beef would appear in various guises such as cottage pie. The meal of tea would follow a pattern, too. For example, on Mondays, Wednesdays, and Fridays, it would be bread and butter with beef dripping (saved from the Sunday roast, eaten with salt), and a mug of milk to drink. Chocolate biscuits would finish the meal. David's menu followed roughly the same simple and repetitive pattern until well into his teens. Many foods taken for granted today were unheard of. David remembers a neighbor saying that she had fed her son a yogurt and the locals were horrified. A strange name must belong to a strange product! If visitors came to tea on a Sunday, they would always be given ham and a salad of lettuce, tomato, and cucumber followed by tinned peaches or mandarin oranges in jelly or small trifles.

Radio played a large part in the routine. Each weekday at 1:45, for example, there was "Listen with Mother" on the BBC radio, fifteen minutes of nursery rhymes and stories for young children. This was followed by "Woman's Hour" which many children were expected to listen to with their mothers at this time. There was no television to watch until 1953 when, along with thousands of other families, the Bebbingtons bought a set to see the coronation of the young Queen Elizabeth. David had his simple toys and was expected to amuse himself for hours at a time while his mother did the housework and cooked. Maybe this was good preparation for later hours of historical research? He still thinks nothing of starting research at 7:30 am, working through to 12:45 p.m. lunch and then continuing from 2 until 6:15, an unusually long span of concentration. And he has never taken coffee breaks! His best friend was "Horsey," a brown stuffed toy. Such was his attachment to "Horsey" that one summer, probably when David was just five, the family discovered on arrival at Bridlington on the Yorkshire coast for their two-week holiday that Horsey had been forgotten and was still in Nottingham. Bill drove straight back to fetch him, a distance of over one hundred miles on poor roads.

David was not exposed to many books in his preschool years. Just three were read and reread to him: *Winnie the Pooh*, *Alice's Adventures in Wonderland*, and *Through the Looking Glass*. Each of these had a profound influence. The first gave him role models to follow, Owl, the lover of long words, and Rabbit, the busy organizer. He still enjoys using unusual words and sometimes says he has had a rabbit sort of day, putting up notices signed Rabbit! The second and third made a rich input into his imagination. When he was asked at primary school to memorize a poem, he naturally chose "Turtle Soup" from *Alice's Adventures in Wonderland*. Birthdays and Christmas provided a break from routine, but Bill and Vera had rather strange ideas about presents. In July 1953, shortly after the first conquest of Mount Everest, David was given for his fourth birthday a complete set of expedition equipment—a sledge, a tent, and so on. Given that it was midsummer and that anything outdoors was regarded in the household as messy and dangerous this seems strange. On another occasion he received boxing gloves from them but David had no one to box with.

One might think this was a healthy childhood, but actually David was often ill. In those days before the widespread use of antibiotics, each bout of illness would require a week or two, the first in bed and the second for a slow recovery. He remembers one illness when, before it, he could not see over the top of the piano and after it he could. By far the most serious was when he had diphtheria when he was just four. This required several weeks in bed and injections every day for a fortnight. This disease was rare by that time in the United Kingdom and could be fatal. Still today, doctors become very interested when they hear of his survival from this illness. That year was not a good year. Vera remembered weeks and weeks of washing only pajamas, never daytime clothes. Eventually when David was almost five, it was decided that his tonsils should be removed. The whole experience was terrifying. Told on the very morning of the operation that it was about to happen, without any preparation, he was left at hospital alone (standard practice in those days) and then heard the nurses discussing the fact that his adenoids were being removed, as well. But no one had mentioned adenoids to David, who had no idea what they were. He tried frantically to tell them that this was a mistake, but no one would listen. He had to stay in the hospital from Wednesday morning until Saturday morning with his parents just visiting at very limited times. When he came out, his face was covered in flaking skin. His face had been smothered in soap each day and he had been left to wash it off with a flannel, but he did not use a flannel at home and so the soap just built up and up. The trauma of that episode remains with him to this day.

Occasionally David would play with his three cousins in Mansfield who were his mother's brother's family, but apart from that he played with virtually nobody his own age before he started school at the age of five. One thing that Vera regarded as her duty was to give the little David a lot of general knowledge and he was encouraged to find out things for himself. Vera regularly asked questions about general knowledge until her death in 1997. She had a thirst for collecting information, another useful habit for the future historian. Strangely the first thing that he can remember his mother collecting was signs from public houses or pubs, odd for a lady who would never darken pub doors. But David was soon on the lookout for new signs for her. These signs were often historical in themselves such as "The Red Lion" or "The Blue Lion," both heraldic animals from the arms of local county families. On the western side of the county was Sherwood Forest. David grew up with the stories of Robin Hood and passed scenes connected with him every time he went to Mansfield. (This was in the time before historians decided that Robin Hood lived in South Yorkshire, some miles to the north! Vera always rejected this slur on the reputation of one of Nottingham's most famous sons.) Another effect that Vera had on him was not so positive; she taught him that the world is a dangerous place, full of physical things to hurt you and trip you up. David was not allowed to play with anything that could conceivably be dangerous in any way and so he was careful to avoid close encounters with the natural world. (This has to have a close connection with his permanent fear of do-it-yourself activities. He is convinced that spanners and screwdrivers are there to harm him.) Also, he was taught that life was a serious business and you needed to be engaged in meaningful activity at all times. You did not take time off to relax.

David was therefore born into patterns and high expectations. He was required to entertain himself for long stretches of time, which has stood him in very good stead for the research part of his career. He quickly came to the conclusion that the physical world was a dangerous place with all sorts of things waiting to harm him. But investigating the wider world of people and places around him, he learned, was a duty and pleasure.

BACKGROUND

So, what patterns of life had brought Bill and Vera to meet in Nottingham? Their story is very much the story of the United Kingdom in the first half of the twentieth century. The First World War, the economic depression of the 1930s, and the Second World War did much to create this world. The Bebbington family had moved down from Barrow-in-Furness because of the slump in ship building immediately after the First World War. Bill's cousins, the Atkinson family, were left in Barrow and a cousin was Mayor of Barrow in the 1950s but visits were not made. David's grandfather, Harold Leach Bebbington, had worked in the Vickers shipyards as a young man but he had moved down to the English Midlands to seek a new job. He became a manager of a firm of builders in Nottingham. With its mixed economy, the city was not affected so badly by the end of the war. Harold was known as a bookish man and it was generally thought that David took after him in this respect, although they never met as Harold had died of leukemia in 1942. A family regret was that Pop did not live to see his book-loving grandson.

Harold and Agnes (née Threlfall) had three children: William or Bill, the eldest and David's father, John Harold, a younger son, and Madge. The family missed the seaside to which they had been used. Bill had led an unrestricted life, roaming for miles. David can remember him reveling in swimming in stormy seas, reliving the pleasures of his youth. Life in Nottingham was more restricted as his mother did not keep well and so Bill became skilled at housekeeping and looking after the rest of the family. He attended High Pavement School, but always regretted that he had not paid enough attention to education. When he left school he became a trainee accountant with the local gas board. He met Vera Urquhart at the Brethren meeting in Nottingham (Brethren are an evangelical Christian group that will be discussed further on) and around ten years later married her in 1939. During the Second World War he was at first classified as having a "reserved occupation"; but in 1942 he was called up and joined the Royal Army Service Corps, rising to become a captain. He was sent to India where troops were massing ready to invade Japan. David has mixed feelings about the atom bomb. If the two bombs had not gone off, hastening the end of the war, his father could well have been killed in the invasion and he would never have existed. Some of the war experiences may have shortened Bill's life. We still have vivid pictures of him in Hiroshima a few months after the nuclear explosion and only after David's father's death did he find out that his father was one of the soldiers forced to watch the experimental atomic explosions in the China Sea on the way home from Japan. Once safely home in 1946, Bill could not bear to be parted from Vera and so he trained as a chiropodist and joined the family business in Mansfield. He worked there until his cancer forced him to stop in 1970. He died in 1971, the day before David's final exams started in Cambridge.

The family chiropody business in Mansfield played an important part in the young David's life. The coal miners of Nottinghamshire often had only Saturdays when their feet could be attended to and so Bill and Vera always worked that day. They took Wednesdays off, but David was at school in later years and so he had very limited time with his father and feels that he never really got to know him. He was long expected to be in bed when his father came home from work. Lack of time meant that all the jobs around the house and garden were done when David was not there. If he did try to do a job, he was nervous and clumsy and could never match his father's prowess. (This has proved something of a challenge in our domestic life. Once after David had been attempting to put up a towel rail, my brother kindly pointed out that he had been trying to drill into the mains water pipe. David retired from DIY very quickly. Somehow, the more he thought about how to do something, the worse his plans became!) Bill felt that he had wasted his education and was determined not to let that happen to his only son. Especially at secondary school he put a lot of pressure on David to succeed and fiercely opposed anything that might deflect him from achieving his potential. Before his third year in the sixth form, aged eighteen, David volunteered to spend two weeks helping with social services, but his father was concerned, thinking that it might divert him from preparing for his Cambridge entrance exams.

The Bebbingtons had not always lived in Barrow. The earliest Bebbingtons that David could find were lords of the manor in Upper Bebington on the Wirral peninsula in northwest England in 1303. They held the lordship in return for the payment of one white rose every St. John's Day. David relishes this link with the fourteenth century. By the seventeenth century the family had come down in the world and were living in the hamlet of Bunbury in the parish of Spurstow in the mid-Cheshire plain, some forty miles from the Wirral. David spent a few days researching the family in Chester County Records Office in 1969 and traced them forwards from 1303 until the early seventeenth century and backwards to the same hamlet in the early eighteenth century but he could not bridge the gap. If he or his cousin John, who has recently been working on the subject, could make the connection, the family would be genuinely entitled to its own coat of arms. Maybe now with so many sources on the internet he will one day manage to achieve this!

The noteworthy event in the family history was the Battle of Flodden in 1513 when the Scots fought the English in the border country between them. It was a dreadful defeat for the Scottish king and the pick of his nobility was slain. Very few English soldiers died, but among them were six Bebbington brothers and their uncle. The "senior line" of the family was almost extinguished. Not only were they killed, but they died running away. They did not want to fight unless under the leadership of their feudal lord, the son of the Earl of Derby, and so they fled at the first Scottish onslaught and paid the price. As David's first professor in Stirling remarked, this argued for "singular military incompetence"!

The Nottingham Years

There was a great deal of Scottish influence on his mother's side. Her maiden name was Urquhart and a painting of Urquhart Castle on Loch Ness in the Scottish Highlands hung on the wall of the Nottingham house. The family came from the Black Isle north of Inverness and Vera's maternal grandmother was a Fraser from Dores on Loch Ness. Her father, Alexander Urquhart, grew up in Carrbridge in Inverness-shire, where his father was the Free Church of Scotland church officer. Alexander (Alec) left for the south coast of England to look for work around the turn of the century, first as a gardener and later as a salesman of miscellaneous goods. Eventually work took him to Nottingham where he attended St. Andrew's Presbyterian Church and met and later married the organist's daughter, Clarice Evelyn Martindale, David's future grandmother. She lived in the West Bridgford area, just over the river Trent from the city of Nottingham, and her father owned a piano and music shop in Arkwright Street, the route into the city center. After marriage they joined the Brethren Assembly in Nottingham and had a son, Roy, and, in 1912, a daughter, Clarice Vera, but always known as Vera, David's mother.

The First World War in 1914 deeply affected the whole family. Alec refused to take up arms and so registered as a conscientious objector. The family became poverty stricken and for some months the small Vera was interned with her father in Roundhay Park in Leeds where he worked on tree management and conditions were primitive. She was then sent to live in Carrbridge in Scotland, where she spent a few happy years surrounded by the lightly wooded, sandy, hilly countryside. She started her education at the tiny Duthil school, which is still there today. Meanwhile her mother and brother went to live with her parents back in Nottingham. At the end of the war Vera was sent south again and remembered a time of having virtually no money and living silently above other people's property where they had no business to be. Job opportunities were nonexistent and so her father decided to go into herbalism and then chiropody, anything to keep them from starving. Vera and her mother went out around Mansfield gathering herbs and drying them to sell in the shop that they rented. Her mother used to tour farms in the area to earn money from her herbs and potions. The father did primitive chiropody training and as a side line they made ice cream under the stairs to sell in the summer. All her life Vera remembered the herbal remedies. She regarded elderflower tea as a cure-all and almost until her death in 1997 would collect and dry elderflowers to use in the winter. These years of extreme poverty left their mark on Vera and her parenting. David still feels deeply troubled if he has to waste food or see it wasted. "Waste not, want not" had been a way to survive, not a platitude.

Alec Urquhart's shop, 11 Belvedere Street, Mansfield

Vera returned after the war to a primary school in Mansfield, but then, when she was eleven, her father was persuaded to pay money he could ill afford to send her to a third-rate private school and Vera's education virtually stopped. (She always blamed that school for ruining her neat handwriting.) Happily, after three years, a new school, High Oakham Girls' Central School, opened near her home and she transferred there. Strangely, as recently as 2005, David picked up a volume of the early issues of bound copies of the High Oakham school magazine, called *Oak Leaves*, in a Derbyshire bookshop he rarely visited and there in the very first issue of 1927 was an article written by his mother about her Scottish experiences entitled "The

The Nottingham Years

County of Inverness, Scotland." There is no doubt that she was very happy living in Carrbridge as a little girl, and David and she drove up there to revisit the area once we had moved to Stirling. More of her memories are in four little books she wrote for her granddaughter before she died. She made up for lost time once she was at High Oakham, but she felt it too late for any real progress. She was expected to join in the family business, in which she had long been involved anyway. Keen to train properly as a chiropodist if she was going to do it at all, she attended a course at the Smae Institute in London. She was extremely popular with patients and specialized in foot massage, similar to reflexology, as well.

Vera's family attended the Brethren meeting in Mansfield and the family ways reflected quite strict restrictions on behavior. For the rest of her life Vera never felt comfortable in a theater or cinema, feeling that the building would collapse and she would be found to have sinned by entering it. Alcohol was strictly banned. Sometimes in the early 1930s Vera visited the central Brethren meeting or assembly in Nottingham and was given hospitality by a Mr. Akroyd, a businessman in the local hosiery industry, and his wife. Gradually she came across the Bebbington family. They asked her home for Sunday lunch and tea before the evening meeting to save her the long journey back to Mansfield and she was immediately attracted to the eldest son, Bill. Her father had other ideas and wanted her to marry somebody else. When he saw that she and Bill were serious, he imposed a seven-year ban on them which they always resented. Eventually Bill and Vera became engaged in 1937 and married in September 1939, just after war broke out. Bill's father gave them a new bungalow as a wedding present at 31 Covedale Road in a street which was just being developed and they lived there together until Bill died of lung cancer in 1971. (Since he was a non-smoker, the exposure to radiation during the war is a likely cause.) Vera died there of heart failure twenty-six years later.

31 Covedale Road, Sherwood, Nottingham

Vera's brother Roy also went into chiropody in Mansfield, but separately from his father. He married David's Auntie Nancy and they had three children, Peter, Keith, and Wendy. David has warm memories of playing with them sometimes, especially at Christmas when they had a huge tree. They were the nearest thing to siblings that he had because Auntie Madge and Uncle Norman (Jones) and family had moved away to Epping and then Cheshire, adding two more children, Kevin and Michael. Occasional visits were the chief contact at that time, but there were also birthday and Christmas presents, one of which was to have lasting significance in David's life. Uncle Harold had married Auntie Janis and had four children, Anne, John, Penny, and Roger, but they lived in Bedford and meetings between the families were rare.

There was one other family of relatives living in Nottingham at that time. Harold Leach Bebbington, David's grandfather, had had an older brother, Sam, who had also moved away from Barrow looking for work. He had gone north to Clydeside in Scotland to become manager in the design department of the famous John Brown shipyards. He was a Brethren lay preacher and when David moved to Stirling in 1976, many people still remembered him. Sam's son, Ernest, became a doctor, as did many educated young Scotsmen at this time, and moving south he became Medical Officer of Health for Beeston, an area next to Nottingham. His son Paul was at the same secondary school as David but five years ahead of him. Many staff assumed they were brothers. Actually the two families virtually never met.

Vera's parents lived in Mansfield in David's early years and her father still worked in the chiropody business. Social visits to them always created strain and David found his grandfather a formidable figure. His grandmother remained a very active lady well into her eighties. Just a few years before she died she wanted David's father to dig an inspection pit in her garage so that she could keep her car in good order. I remember feisty conversations in the early 1970s with her about the women's liberation movement.

This then was the background into which David was born. Life was not expected to be easy and self-reliance was at a premium. There was a strong expectation that you would not be scared to be different, you would stand up for your principles and you would not be affected by peer pressure. It was a recipe for nonconformity.

EDUCATION

In September 1954, David started at Seely Primary School. It was located in the local council estate, a public housing area in Sherwood, the part of Nottingham where the family lived. The school was one mile away from his home, down and then up very steep hills. David walked this route from the age of just five. The early walking with his mother had prepared him well. It seems extraordinary now that a small child was expected to travel this far on foot, but there was no "school run" in those days. Any family car would be used to take the breadwinner, usually the father, to work. No one would have dreamed of dropping off children at school. To start with, David's mother went with him to school, but very soon he was expected to make the journey four times a day on his own. The one word that he uses to describe his first year at school is "terrified." He had previously met very few children of his own age. The strange environment, being thrown into the company of so many other children for the first time, seemed overwhelming. He cried not only at the start of the first term but also at the beginning of the two subsequent terms. Vera had been a serious mother, intent on speaking the truth at all times. David had never been teased before and so was an easy target to upset. Nowadays it could be called bullying. One favorite method was to tell him that there was a nuclear bomb in the gutter which was about to explode. Some of Vera's anxiety rubbed off on David and throughout his school life he found academic tests and doing the right thing causes of worry. His parents had tried to prepare him for his first day by sending him for a practice day to the primary school of a neighbor who was a headmistress. David remembers lukewarm milk that was meant to be cold and cubed carrots which were the "wrong shape" for lunch. His parents were told that he had coped well with the day, but he had actually felt bored and anxious. At the end of the first day of his own school his parents took him on a picnic because it was a Wednesday, his father's day off. David felt that school might be bearable if a picnic came at the end of each day, but sadly he found this never happened again and he felt let down. Another anxiety was that on Tuesdays after school he had to go to one of two homes of other pupils for tea because his mother had returned to work in Mansfield. One of the houses contained an advent calendar before Christmas and this bothered the small boy who had been taught that the church year with its divisions such as advent was a diversion from biblical truth.

Seely Primary School Assembly Hall

Vera's teaching of general knowledge and encouragement of finding out things for himself had made David an especially well-informed little boy. For his sixth birthday his Mansfield cousins gave him a world atlas, which he devoured with enthusiasm. In the second year at school he told the teacher where the Minch and the Little Minch channels were in the north of Scotland on a map of Britain. So unusual was this geographical expertize that he was sent to the headmistress to tell her, too. David showed very early signs that not only did he like acquiring information but he also liked classifying it. He learned to read very quickly and remembers that almost as soon as he started school he copied out, with some difficulty, the "Plan to Catch a Baby Roo" from *Winnie the Pooh*, Tigger's plan of action to rid the forest of Kanga, a new arrival. This scheme appealed greatly to David; several months later he copied it out again and realized that he could now do it much more easily. Never allowed to be precocious, at home he was always expected to collect information. The school catered for his tastes, teaching Homer's *Odyssey* to his second-year class when he was six (though his father was worried that this work of the imagination was not proper history). Yet it took several years for him to integrate into the school. Classes were big by today's standards, with more than forty being the regular size.

If education means training in life, then the town of Mansfield played a large part in David's education. On Saturdays and in school holidays he had to go to Mansfield all day with his parents and that meant sitting in the surgery where the chiropody was taking place. For part of the day he would take toys to play with quietly, but from the age of five, if not sooner, he was allowed to go "round the block" as long as he did not cross a road. He was sent along to a shop round the corner to buy the "ham off the bone" for lunch. The block opened up a whole new world to him including a "cut through" to its other side. To this day he loves alleyways and cut-throughs, especially in towns being explored for the first time. Mansfield was his playground, his world of adventure and his education. Once he was seven he was allowed anywhere in the town. He soon learned how to enjoy long periods in the shops without spending money and the legacy of that experience is with him until today. Unlike the male stereotype, he is an enthusiastic and excellent shopper. Nowadays it would be unheard of for a small child to wander the shops alone for hours at a time. David particularly loved the open market in Mansfield where "Dutch auctions" would go on for half an hour at a time in which a stall holder attracted a crowd around and then tried to persuade some of them to buy some of his amazing goods for a so-called bargain price. The local Woolworths store remains in David's memory as being full of excitement. The wooden counters, the polished floor, the shiny range of Christmas decorations all entranced the small observer. He feels he learned useful skills there. With this love of classifying information, he did some research on manufacturers of washing powder (detergent). He was intrigued to discover that Procter and Gamble had an almost total monopoly in this field! This was his very own first research project. Sadly the Mansfield of his youth is no longer there. The branch of

Woolworths has disappeared because its parent company recently ceased trading. Much of the central part of the town was demolished in the 1970s to build an inner ring road, including a wonderful Quaker meeting house that David had always loved, and even the chiropody surgery has gone.

On Wednesdays, he might go with his parents in school holidays to the center of Nottingham. The city was flourishing, with many hosiery factories still in business and the two main employers, Raleigh bicycles and Players cigarettes, in full production. Boots the chemist was in the ascendancy. Again the market, with its variety of stalls, appealed to him, but here as well were seriously large shops with huge ranges of everything you could need. The family often shopped at the large stores of the time, long before the modern Victoria Centre was built: Griffin and Spalding, Pearsons, and Jessops. From the age of six, David was a regular user of the local buses. His first trip by himself was to the local postage stamp shop in Hyson Green, a ride of around ten minutes. Fascinated by the exotic name on the stamp, he bought a large pre-First World War stamp from Bosnia-Herzegovina. David used the city buses to travel to school until he left Nottingham. In fact he found the cigarette-smoke-filled atmosphere unpleasant and only his senior bus travel card is beginning to convert him to bus use again! The pre-Christmas period again was one of excitement and if Christmas Eve fell on a Wednesday it was spent on a shopping trip into town. For these special trips the family car would always be used. Vera had driven since the age of seventeen, which was the legal age of driving. There was no such thing as a driving test in those days. And Bill and Vera had a car from before the time David was born, first an Austin 30 which David loved. He was sad when they upgraded to an Austin 40. He even classified the colors of the cars on the road. Most cars were still black, but colored cars were just coming into fashion and he imagined a sustained warfare between black and colored vehicles. The A30 was a pale pink color and he felt that it was a very modern car compared with the black.

David remained at Seely School until around his eleventh birthday. In his final year he was boys' captain of the school. He greatly enjoyed the school carol service in the local parish church, where he read one of the poems and was consulted by the teacher about the correct pronunciation of ecclesiastical Latin even though he did not know the language at that stage: for some reason it was supposed that he would have the answer! In his last year he was commended for supporting football practice, though football was (according to his school report) a sport "at which he does not excel." He never completely recovered from the fear of his early days there and always felt pressure.

In Nottingham in the early 1960s, a time of major decision in a child's education came at the age of eleven. All pupils sat an "11 plus" examination to decide whether they should go on to grammar school or to a more practically orientated secondary modern school. At that time Nottingham had a lowish rate of pupils going on to grammar school, roughly 20 percent as against a national average of 25 percent for England. A few of the top performers were selected to go to the two private schools where they would have their fees paid for them by the City or County Council. David sat the exam in the spring of 1960, answering questions in English and arithmetic and taking intelligence tests which were meant to pick up academic potential. The math questions still strike fear into his heart today. They were very much of the type "If it takes three men fourteen days to dig a trench, how long would it take seven and a half men to dig it?" or "If one train leaves A at 4:30 and travels at 50 mph, when would it meet a second train that left B at 5:15 and traveled at 60 mph?" It turned out that David was one of the two top boys in the 11 plus from all the Nottingham city primary schools and was awarded an All Saints' Scholarship at Nottingham High School from September 1960. He had sat the school entrance exam, but this was geared to the boys in the preparatory department who had had more sophisticated preparation. David was expected to write an essay on myxomatosis, a deadly disease in rabbits. He had no idea what that word meant so could not perform well!

The High School, founded by Dame Agnes Mellers in 1513 for the sons of the people of Nottingham, provided David with an excellent education but also with an environment where history was all around him. David was in a form (or class) of city and county scholarship boys and enjoyed most of the new subjects—Latin, French, religious knowledge, history, geography, English, math, and science, which on the whole were very well taught. Some subjects had specialist teachers who nowadays would be in a university rather than in a school, but these were the days before the expansion of higher education. The form master in his first year, Geoffrey Cushing, a young man who had recently graduated from Cambridge, was an ideal mentor. He was an able Latin teacher and also had to take scripture (religious knowledge), as all form masters were expected to do. He was an active Methodist local preacher and so having a Christian faith seemed natural. He was later to become a headmaster elsewhere. Dick

Elliott, David's second-year form master and Latin teacher, brought his classical knowledge to the scripture lessons and so enriched Bible background with his classical history. Christian teaching permeated the school. Indeed, Bill and Vera were told by the headmaster at the very start that he was committed to giving the boys a Christian education. The head of religious knowledge, Frank Collander-Brown, a spiritual and compassionate man, had been headmaster of Monkton Combe Preparatory School in the 1930s. The most outstanding teacher was Dr. I. C. Thimann who, as head of modern languages, taught David French in his first year. (His brother Dr. Eric Thimann was organist at the City Temple Congregational Church in London and had close links to my family.) Dr. Thimann, the teacher who remained David's tutor, responsible for monitoring his progress throughout the school, expected a lot from his pupils and David enjoyed the challenge. Half-way through the first term, overall form positions based on academic results in every subject were calculated. David remembers being amazed when Geoffrey Cushing said that he was expecting David to be top of the form. (He wasn't, he came second!) He had no idea at all whether he was very good or just good at some things. Each term after that there were form lists, ranked by achievement, taken up to the headmaster at morning assembly by each top boy. (David did this in the second and third term.) The lists spurred him on to harder work. The poorest teaching was in science and so his awareness of scientific patterns was meagre. In fact, science was never linked to patterns at all. The text books were fat, unreadable tomes. First-year science was not too bad, but the second year was awful. Everyone was amused when the teacher went off to be a university lecturer!

The Nottingham Years

Nottingham High School

The school quickly gave David a structured alternative life parallel to home. He had already been taught that he should stand up when talking to older people, but at the High School he learned to touch his cap in the street (the headgear was compulsory) to the masters and to any women whom he knew. He had a half day on Thursday, but had lessons every Saturday morning until lunchtime. Maybe this is why he is still much happier working on a Saturday morning at the university, feeling strangely guilty if he does not. Because his parents worked all day on Saturday, he became involved in sports activities on Saturday afternoons. He had a brief career as hooker in the Under-15 school rugby team. He has memories of traveling by coach to local minor public schools and can still remember whether the tea they were given was good or inedible. His career in the rugby team came to an abrupt end once they were being encouraged to cheat in the scrum and he quickly joined the school library staff in preference. There he experienced working with one of the most satisfying of all the patterns of his life: the Dewey Decimal System of classification. This method for arranging books on library shelves was designed to categorize the whole of life. He remembers being amused that radio was allocated a really obscure number, 621.3841. By the second year of the sixth form he was in charge of the library with a staff of thirty or so other boys under him to run it. But he also became one of the scorers for the athletics teams and spent happy Saturday afternoons traveling to away matches in Nottinghamshire and Derbyshire. Another choice in fourth year would have been to join the Combined Cadet Force to practice army, navy and air force skills, but he was happy to escape to the school library instead. From fourth year on David acted as school Concert Manager and school Play Manager and from fifth year he organized the Penguin Bookshop, all of which entailed substantial responsibilities almost entirely beyond staff supervision. All these jobs provided him with excellent administrative experience.

Gradually in the first five years at the school he worked towards "Ordinary Level" examinations (run by the Oxford and Cambridge Examinations Board), taking three subjects (English language, elementary math, and French) in fourth year, aged fourteen, and seven others (history, English literature, Latin, advanced math, general science, religious knowledge, and geography) in his fifth year in 1965. Strangely the school had a practice of not telling pupils how they had done and so to this day David does not know his O level results. All he knows is that his geography result was the highest in the country for that exam board. When forms had to be completed for university applications the school filled in the results after the pupils had completed the rest. For Advanced levels David chose history, English and Roman history with Latin translation. His A level results at the age of seventeen were three Grade As, but with an A1 in English and an A2 in history, which was ironic as by now he knew he wanted to do history.

As was then the standard practice, David remained at school for a third year in the sixth form in order to take the Cambridge entrance exam. The time came for university applications. The school had long sent someone every year to Jesus College to read history and in his year David was selected to apply. His third choice was Durham, which offered him a place and where he still feels he would have been very happy. The second was Manchester, which had a very high reputation for history at the time. Much to his parents' annoyance, he had not been made a prefect at the start of the second-year sixth, but David appreciates that decision because he did not have people skills at that time. He was duly appointed later and became house captain from late in the second-year sixth, organizing the winning of the inter-house music competition in the following year like a military campaign. In his last year he had intended to leave school at Christmas 1967 and work in the City Library until his Cambridge course started, but instead he returned to school and carried out a huge variety of administrative jobs. He even worked out the school timetable for the following year. His parents hoped he would read law, but the pull of history was too strong. As it turned out, Jesus College awarded him an exhibition, an award of

£40 a year which originally was almost enough to fund a year's study at Cambridge, but now paid only for a few books, and so in October 1968, at the age of nineteen, he became an undergraduate at Jesus College.

David has always been grateful for the education and experience he received at Nottingham High School. He was encouraged to work very hard and to pursue new areas of knowledge. This pattern was now ingrained in him. The quality of teaching was very high in most subjects and the experience of running the annual concert, organizing the school library and even preparing the whole school timetable in his final year stood him in good stead for the future. He has long thought that he could have gone into the civil service and pursued a career in public administration if history had not pulled him so hard. School was not always easy. He was under huge pressure from home to achieve his best and the competition in his form was intense. He had never felt at ease fitting in socially. The legacy from his earliest years never went away. He took life very seriously and this did not always go down well among his contemporaries. He adopted some coping strategies like walking backwards around the school yard, carrying several briefcases of books simultaneously and wearing extremely long raincoats! He still made it a habit to use unusual words. But he made some good friends. At the start of the school holidays he would try to fix times to meet others during the coming weeks and was surprised when other boys did not know what they were doing a month ahead. With Gordon Waller, who was to become his best man at his wedding, he would go out in the countryside visiting parish churches. The High School must have been one of the best schools in the country at the time.

THE CHRISTIAN FAITH

For the first eight years of his life, David was taken to the Brethren assembly in Aspley, then on the outskirts of Nottingham. The Brethren are a Christian group who believe in "gathering together" into local assemblies without any central organization. Each assembly organizes itself and is run by the elders or "oversight." At the morning meeting the communion service would be central with men offering prayers or delivering a word from the Lord as they were led. At the evening meeting one of the men would lead the meeting and the stress would be on the need for personal salvation. The expectation of being different, a "little flock" (the title of the hymn book in use at Aspley), meant that David was left with a legacy of never minding standing out from the crowd or being afraid to be different. His paternal grandfather had helped create the new assembly at Aspley in the 1930s. There had been several generations of Brethren in the family. David's great-grandfather had helped found the assembly in Barrow. Before this, as has recently been discovered by John Bebbington, the great-great-grandfather had been a retained Primitive Methodist preacher in Cheshire, which may explain David's deep interest in the denomination. He remembers the reverence with which the communion service ("the breaking of bread") was treated and to this day has a very high regard for the Lord's Supper, loving to celebrate it every week.

When David was nine, however, his parents moved to Queensberry Street Baptist Church in Old Basford, an old industrial village incorporated in the city of Nottingham. Here the whole family enjoyed the ministry of the Reverend Glyn Morris; the families became friendly and Mr. Morris was to pray at our wedding in 1971. At Queensberry it was always stressed that each person had to make a personal decision about becoming a Christian. About a year after starting to worship in this church, a lady preached who was from the Pocket Testament League, an evangelical society committed to the use of small pocket-sized gospels for telling people the good news about Jesus. At the door after the service, she asked David if he was a Christian and he said he was not, a remarkably frank reply. So she recommended that he should go home, follow the steps in one of the testaments and commit his life to Jesus, which is exactly what he did. It was on June 19, 1960. He went through to tell his parents in tears and still feels that it was a real conversion experience. His faith continued to grow through the work of Sunday school and then Junior Church on a Sunday afternoon. This did make Sundays pretty full. The family would attend the morning service at 10:45, go home for lunch, David and his father would be at Junior Church for 2:15, go home for a quick tea, and then, with Vera, return for evening service at 6:15. No wonder he feels deprived if he cannot manage at least two services on a Sunday! Although believer's baptism normally followed conversion, David waited to be baptized. Wise Junior Church leaders allowed him a certain amount of latitude. At one point he was given three consecutive Sunday afternoons to lead the group on the study of the Apocrypha, in which he particularly enjoyed Bel and the Dragon.

THE NOTTINGHAM YEARS

Queensberry Street Baptist Church, Old Basford, Nottingham

At the same time the High School did much to expand his faith. As we have seen, each master had to teach religious education and this responsibility was taken very seriously. The syllabus up to O level was a more thorough grounding in the Bible than many theological colleges would now give, going through the whole of the New Testament and the Old, early church history and then, for the few volunteering for the national O level exam, in-depth studies of Mark's gospel and the prophets Jeremiah and Ezekiel. Sometimes he assumes that everyone has had a similar grounding, which can be difficult at times! The RE teaching was led by Frank Collander-Brown, an excellent scholar of New Testament Greek. The school choir contributed new depth, with Bach chorales and the Fauré Requiem. He sang in the choir until his voice broke at the start of the fourth year. Also he owes a lot to the Christian Discussion Group (CDG), which brought him into contact with Christians of various denominations. In the sixth form he had many heated discussions with his Methodist friend Andrew Sails, son of the minister of Nottingham Methodist Mission and subsequently himself a minister, and established his theological grounding at this time. The CDG visited a wide range of places of worship such as the Catholic Cathedral and the Quaker meeting, which again enriched his experience. In 1965 a Brethren speaker came to the CDG and spoke about the pattern of timing in his Sunday morning meetings and David decided to time what happened in any service he attended. That was the start of his taking notes on services, a practice which has continued until now.

The daily school assemblies contributed to the overall Christian content of his life. This was the time when the *Honest to God* debate was raging, in which Bishop John Robinson was arguing that God is to be found in the depth of our being rather than as an external reality. In the radical theological atmosphere of the times, several visiting speakers at school assembly treated Christianity very much as social action, "doing things" rather than the "believing things" that was emphasized at church. This set up a tension for David. In the third-year sixth Gordon Waller passed on to him a book about the Congregational theologian P. T. Forsyth, who stressed the centrality of the cross and the redemptive work of the atonement. Forsyth had decided that the work of Jesus on the cross was at the heart of Christianity. This helped David enormously. It set the text that was in large letters at the front of Queensberry Street Baptist Church, "We Preach Christ Crucified," in a reflective theological context and helped to reconcile the Christianity of home and school.

The writings of Paul Tillich also helped in resolving the dilemma about "doing" and "believing." Tillich wrote about "The New Being" that is the essence of Christianity. One evening coming back from a prefects' party at school, David had a spiritual experience when a street light appeared to glow brightly just as the burning bush did for Moses in the wilderness. A lot of things clicked into place for him. To Moses, God declared himself to be "I am that I am." If God is fundamentally *being*, then that is what Christians are to be, too. Believing things and doing things, affirmations and actions, are of equal importance but both flow from *being* something. The result was a Trinitarian schema of being, affirming, and doing, corresponding to Father, Son, and Holy Spirit. That was the foundation for David's first sermon, attended by several of his school friends, at a Baptist church in Hyson Green in the spring of 1968, and remains the formulation of faith that he finds most satisfying. Happier now, David was baptized at his Nottingham church on Whit Sunday 1968. The hymn "Come Down, O Love Divine" was sung, and the stage was set for his faith to develop further at Cambridge.

Shortly after the baptism David attended the very first Baptist Historical Society Summer School at Spurgeon's College in South London and experienced the wider Baptist denomination. Dr. Ernest Payne, who had been the general secretary of the Baptist Union of Great Britain and Ireland, as well as then serving as a vice president of the World Council of Churches, took a kindly interest in this eager young man and even sat with him on the bus tour, which gave David a great deal of encouragement. At the time when he went up to Cambridge in October 1968, David was reading an article by Dr. Payne which included comment on the views of Charles Simeon, the Cambridge divine of around the start of the nineteenth century. Simeon was convinced that truth lay in both extremes ("both . . . and"), not in one or the other and certainly not somewhere in between. Once again this formula helped David to reconcile the two different types of Christianity that he had experienced most closely. He went up to Cambridge with a level of theological understanding that was unusual.

HISTORY

In his earliest years, history was present in David's life through trips to view great houses, which his parents enjoyed visiting. Neither of them had received much formal education, but outings such as these were part of the routine on days off. They were always keen to remember becoming engaged to be married at Belvoir Castle, which stands on a striking cliff overlooking the Vale of Belvoir in Leicestershire, not far from Nottingham. At the age of four David made his first visit to a stately home in southwest Nottinghamshire. The first decisive historical influence was a book given to him on his seventh birthday by his Auntie Madge, his father's sister. It was a history of England in the Middle Ages and contained text and pictures about knights and castles. He started his own collection of model knights and horses and remains very particular about the accuracy of the heraldry on toy knights, carefully examining modern ones in toy shops to check for authenticity. A year or two later his father built him a splendid medieval-style model castle. The knight collection then had a home, but had to be kept out of sight of his noncombatant grandfather. In the year when he was nine, group projects were introduced at school for the first time and his group was given the subject of the early development of Nottingham from the Saxon times of the fifth and sixth centuries through the Norman period and into the industrial era. Nottingham was a perfect example of a city that was large enough for buildings from the different periods to be seen. David remains to this day a highly urban-loving person. He certainly threw himself into this project with a will. His mother helped him find press cuttings and other pieces of information. In this way his interest in local history began. (It is interesting to speculate how his life would have developed if he had been given "how steam engines work" instead.) Once David had learned about the city, he became very excited to discover that the Old Market Square in the city center, which he had assumed always to have been the focus, was actually an eleventh-century Norman addition tacked on to the earlier Anglo-Saxon center in what is now the Lace Market. A sense of change over time was developing.

We think that the teacher must have seen his enthusiasm, because in the next term for an individual project he suggested that David should do something on the ancient world. From this came David's very first book (which we still have!). The title was *A History of the Ancient World with Which Is Incorporated Classical Mythology*. It has four volumes and is complete with footnotes. (He still does not regard a book as "proper" without footnotes, the more the better.) The elaborate title definitely betrays the influence of Wol in his thinking. The writing was on the wall about the shape of his future career. The teacher lent him a classic book on the ancient world by an American author, J. H. Breasted, called *Ancient Times: A History of the Early World*, originally published in the 1916, as his main source. Imposing order on information was emerging as something David loved to do and he was discovering more and more ways of doing it. In the school projects he sorted, categorized, and placed material in order. He was beginning to make particular patterns of his own.

Before he started at Nottingham High School, his parents attended a meeting in the school at the end of the previous summer term which was to supply information for the following school year. They saw a history of the school for sale and so they bought it, knowing that David would enjoy it. By the time he started in the September, he had read and assimilated the material in the book (including the footnotes). He found it very strange that everyone had not done the same. Over the next eight years he reveled in the historic associations of the school. He especially enjoyed the annual

The Nottingham Years

Founder's Day, when on a Saturday in June the whole school would process from the current buildings a mile north of the city center to St. Mary's Parish Church in the Lace Market for a commemorative service.

History at the High School was mind-expanding compared with what he had done at Seely. But excitingly David discovered that history had many uses. At the start of the second year in English, members of the form were asked to write about what they had done in the holidays and so David was able to write about the two weeks he had spent in North Wales, visiting the castles of King Edward I. It was the first time that he realized that history could be useful in other subjects as well. He later found this in O level geography when he was asked to write about the Fens of East Anglia. He combined his historical and geographical knowledge to explain the monastic origins of fen drainage from the Middle Ages. In his first year at the High School he had become a member of the school history society although it was designed for older boys, and subsequently he joined the Thoroton Society, the local historical society in Nottingham. He attended its Saturday afternoon talks and went on its trips financed willingly by his father, often with groups of older lady enthusiasts. The society had its own headquarters in the Old Market Square with a library of Nottinghamshire books, a sort of club room where David would meet likeminded friends. In these various ways, David was able to develop a deep knowledge and love of local history.

School history gave him a very thorough grounding. In the five years before O Levels, his classes studied in the first year the Romans and up to the end of the Middle Ages, in the second Tudors and Stuarts, in the third ancient history and civics, in the fourth, which was the start of the public exam syllabus, the eighteenth and early nineteenth centuries, and in the fifth year the nineteenth century. No twentieth-century history was taught as it was not yet regarded as a valid subject. In the two years of the sixth form the syllabus was entirely on the medieval period and general historical essays. This reflected the medieval interests of the two history masters. The senior master was Dr. Adam Thomas, who had left Oxford in the early 1930s and taught in a fairly traditional way, which suited David. The other was David Peters, whom some pupils found dry but whose teaching David enjoyed. The classics master Dick Elliott was a classical historian and taught David to cut to the nub of any issue, which he tries to do in seminars to this day.

Alongside David's school-based studies went a growing interest in architecture and heraldry. In the first year at the High School, Dr. Thomas told the class that serious historians should study parish churches with their wealth of medieval architecture. David was already used to looking at old buildings on his trips and holidays but now he became keener on churches. By the fifth and sixth year it had become a serious hobby and his appreciation of the Pevsner *Buildings of England* series came in. He would visit churches with three guide books: the *Little Guide* to the county, Arthur Mee's *Counties of England* local volume, and the relevant Pevsner guide. By the time we met in 1968 he would spend a great deal of time trying to spot errors in the Pevsner guides, but I swiftly discouraged that as a hobby.

Another result of the way in which history was taught was the development of David's own shorthand which he has used ever since. Large chunks of notes were dictated to the boys and David wanted to take down every word. He found that if he did so he would remember most of what had been said without referring to the notes. He still uses this method to take down what is said at lectures he attends. Apart from giving him something to do if the speaker is a little tedious at times, as a result he can usually remember what has been said very clearly. This meant that at exam times he could build on these notes. He did not have to go over and over them to try to make his brain remember them. This helped a great deal and enabled him to fit the information into patterns of argument very quickly. And so the shorthand developed. All his research notes, his sermon and service notes and everything else is written in this personal way—the only slight problem being that there is no written key to it anywhere!

TRIPS AND GEOGRAPHY

Although we have explored David's interest in history first because of his subsequent career, we probably should have looked at trips and geography before that. As long as he can remember, David was taken on days out, often to local stately homes. They gave him a much-needed break from routine. Much of David's home life as a young boy consisted of hard, regular work and routine. His parents worked five days a week from 8:15 a.m. to 5:45 p.m. With church several times on a Sunday, there were no opportunities for trips out during a normal week. However, there was a regular pattern of holidays and bank holidays when there was a chance for the members of the family to leave Nottingham. In David's early years, a typical destination might be the beautiful Peak District of Derbyshire, where they might walk along by a river, but he was also taken to historic spots such as Ingestre Hall in Staffordshire or Kenilworth Castle in Warwickshire. These breaks from routine became dominant in his thinking and a lifeline for him. The first holiday of the year was Good Friday, immediately before Easter Sunday, and then his parents would always take the Monday, Tuesday, and Wednesday off as well. Then there would be a chance for three trips at the late Spring Bank Holiday which used to be at Whitsuntide, seven weeks after Easter. There would be three days over the August Bank Holiday weekend at the start of August. Before long, David would be planning these days of escape meticulously, balancing different destinations for different days with adjustments possible for variations in the weather. This became a very early example of David being able to develop a pattern. He used the technique for summer holidays as well. He very much enjoyed a Cornish holiday in 1960 and one based at Llandudno in 1961, which started his lifelong affection for Wales, its people, its history, and especially its daffodils. Our garden in spring reflects this attachment. He has now visited many places at home and abroad but he still feels genuinely on holiday only when in Wales. The summer holiday that was most carefully planned was one based in Scarborough in 1964, with visits to medieval abbeys taking pride of place.

David aged about 15 with his father on holiday

As with history, the geography syllabus at school was thorough and David found more and more that he could intertwine history with geography. He wished he could have taken geography as a fourth A level subject, actually investigating the possibility, but it would have been impractical. He rested content with taking an enduring interest in the geographical setting of events past and present.

BOOKS, BUSES, BOARD GAMES AND BOOK COLLECTING

Before he went to school David did not encounter many books. As we have said, the three that were read to him were *Winnie the Pooh*, *Alice's Adventures in Wonderland*, and *Through the Looking Glass*. His parents possessed some books to do with their faith, but they did not interest the small boy. No attempt was made to teach him to read before he started school, but he must have picked the habit up very quickly from the *Janet and John* readers (which he remembers as very tedious) as by seven he was reading Sir Walter Scott's *Ivanhoe*, a daunting prospect for any reader in the twenty-first century. His rather stern grandmother told him to read the Bible, and so he started at Genesis and reached the book of Job. He thought it was pronounced *job*, as in "Bob-a-Job Week" and so could see no sense in it. So ended the read through! A new branch library opened in Sherwood at this stage and for a while he was taken to it in order to choose books to borrow. The novelty soon wore off and regular library borrowing from a public library was not to start again until he was sixteen. He read various books connected with school projects and during the final year of primary school it acquired a library, designed to enhance the quality of the education. Unfortunately the school was so proud of the beautifully displayed books that all the pupils were forbidden to touch them! At the start of the High School, however, he soon visited the school library and was delighted that the volumes of the second edition of Thoroton's *Antiquities of Nottinghamshire*, published in 1790, were available for borrowing. He kept one or other at home for most of the first year.

At the top of the primary school David became friendly with a boy who played board games such as Totopoly and Scoop. He invited David to play with him and his friend and thus began David's lifelong love of board games. Not only did he play them, but he started to collect them and also to make up his own. His parents still worked on Saturdays and he was expected to occupy himself all day. So after exhausting the thrills of

The Nottingham Years

Woolworths and the market he would sit and invent board games. The first one was imitative of Totopoly and then he went on to design one about the planets and one about the American Civil War, all drawn on blue cardboard from his parents' supplies in the surgery. He still believes that he could have marketed them and maybe made his fortune but never got round to it! One of the problems was that they were never ending, which was no problem when you had all day to play. I am not sure he has ever become used to playing with another real person. As he grew older he enjoyed Diplomacy, a game which reproduced the power politics of Europe on the eve of the First World War and which could last several hours or days. He also played the simpler and quicker game of Nine Men's Morris, which he was once delighted to find inscribed on the threshold of a medieval abbey.

Television was the major relaxation pursuit in the household and David is an authority on programs from *Watch with Mother* to the first episode of *Coronation Street*, a long-running soap opera! His parents would watch TV all evening and so would David while still at primary school, when he had no homework to do. By the age of fourteen he was not reading anything for pleasure and so his father persuaded him to read the Poirot novels of Agatha Christie. He has not stopped reading since! He reads on buses, planes, and trains. He reads in doctors' and dentists' waiting rooms. He reads whenever possible. This used to confuse me, but then we discovered that Mr. Gladstone (of whom more later) did exactly the same and so that gave the practice validation!

Along with the board games came the bus number collecting phase. In the second year at Nottingham High School, David would take himself off around the area to bus stations where he could collect bus numbers. Derby, Chesterfield and other centers could produce more numbers than just Nottingham. And so David could plan trips which he organized for himself in order to collect information to classify. This he feels was an important forerunner to the book-collecting methods of the last forty-five years.

Having collected board games, he found it a natural progression to move on to collecting books. During his family holiday in Scarborough on the Yorkshire coast in 1964, David went into a secondhand book shop for something to do and bought a Morley's *Life of Gladstone* in three volumes. Little did he know that fifty years later he would still be using that book to teach students in Stirling and Texas. In 1965 he was given money to go to London for his sixteenth birthday and so he "did" the bookshops of the Charing Cross Road, including Foyles, an amazing shop packed with books on several floors. He could have been there at the same time as me, since as that was my favorite shop in London at the time. But for day-to-day purposes, and it was daily, Ian Cowley's bookshop on the Mansfield Road in Nottingham was crucial. Situated close to the school bus stop, it was a warm, happy place to browse rather than go home to an empty house. Ian Cowley knew his trade well and David started collecting a few books in many different fields, though soon specializing in Nottinghamshire books. From these small beginnings have come the visits to secondhand bookshops across the world.

SUMMARY

So which of David's later traits were clear by this time? In the two worlds of his family and the school he had developed his love of trips and geography. From his earliest years he had been interested not just in acquiring information but also in organizing it into patterns. History was well established, book collecting had started and he had written the first book of his own. Heraldry and ecclesiology were prominent, but they do not feature largely now because his historical interests have moved on from the Middle Ages. His Christian faith was well established. From his Brethren background came the requirement to be different and to stand up for your principles. How then did these traits develop in Cambridge?

2

The Cambridge Years

EDUCATION

The move to university in Cambridge proved to be far less of a shock for David than for many because of the high numbers of boys from his school already there or "going up" at the same time. He went with twenty-seven others from his year, something of a record. Roughly 1 percent of the university at that time came from Nottingham High School. He loved the sheer antiquity of his college, whose full title was the College of the Blessed Virgin Mary, St. John the Evangelist and the Glorious Virgin St. Radegund, commonly known as Jesus College, Cambridge. Founded in the late fifteenth century on the site of a nunnery, the college had buildings ranging from the Cloister Court of the twelfth century to the modern 1960s one. The unusual entrance, with its long approach between two walls, was known as the Chimney. As an exhibitioner, David had three rooms of his own in 12CC1 in Chapel Court, a kitchen, a bedroom, and a keeping or sitting room with a sofa, table, and bookcases opening off a small hall. Chapel Court was a relatively modern building designed around 1930 by the architect Morley Horder. Almost incredibly today, the rooms had no bathroom or toilet. These facilities were not even at the end of the corridor but down some very steep stairs to an underground area which could be quite gloomy, especially after a depressed student hanged himself down there in David's first year. Even more extraordinary was the lack of heating, with only an ancient popping gas fire in the keeping room and none at all in the kitchen or bedroom, which was hard in the icy Cambridge winters when the wind was said to blow straight from the Ural mountains in Russia across the wonderful flat

East Anglian countryside. Central heating had not reached Chapel Court, but since it was only just being installed in the Nottingham house, this was not strange for the time. Each undergraduate was assigned to a tutor whom he met once a term to check on how he was doing generally. The tutors had nothing to do with academic work unless someone was really struggling. Evening meals were taken in hall after a Latin grace had been said. Customs could seem a little primitive to visitors, with undergraduates climbing over tables to get out from beside the ancient walls where they had been sitting on backless benches.

Jesus College, Cambridge

David threw himself into many sorts of activities, all of which were connected to his historical or Christian interests. He joined the Cambridge Heraldic and Genealogical Society which met three times a term and the Ecclesiology Society where he soon joined the committee. Later the college history society came into being and he was secretary of that. He visited friends from school and organized the university old boys' dinner. The Christian Union in college held a weekly Bible study and on a Saturday evening a "Bible Reading" was held where he heard some great speakers such as the Reverend John Stott. Not a lot of work got done that first year, but he was experiencing different activities. Some stand out. There were sometimes invitations to join fellows of the college, that is senior academics, for drinks or meals. As a provincial boy he had never even heard of anchovies. When asked to breakfast by one senior don, thinking they were a type of small sardine, he put a large helping of them on his toast. He has not recovered since! It would be hard not to feel aware of the tradition of the college when alumni included the poet Samuel Taylor Coleridge and in more recent years Alistair Cooke, whose historical studies at the college became the background for his many years of broadcasting *Letter from America*. It was around this time that David began to keep his "little black book" or commonplace book. He had been reading about a nineteenth-century artisan who had started a collection of quotations late in life and wished he had started earlier. Into David's black book went all sorts of amusing, interesting, and unusual statements which could be drawn on at various social occasions or at times when he was suddenly asked to "say a few words." This extra item did create pressure on his pockets which already held his small file of lists of things to do. He has never regretted starting this practice and now has a series of these books.

The Cambridge academic year ran from early October until early June. There were three terms, Michaelmas, Lent, and Easter, of eight weeks each. An extra term in the summer called Long Vac(ation) Term gave a chance for more study and David was able to enjoy it free in 1970 because by then he was a scholar of the college. The University "Tripos" examinations were divided into two parts, Part 1 and Part 2. History students took Part 1 after two years and Part 2 after their final third year. College exams were held at the end of first year but did not count towards the final result. Eight weeks may seem short for a university term, but so much was packed into them that they became the equivalent of a much longer experience. There were endless opportunities for discussion, debate, musical activities of all sorts, plays, and social gatherings. These were heady days politically. The Garden House Riot was to take place in Cambridge in February 1970 when students protested against the then regime in Greece. This had followed on from major student riots in Paris in 1968. When the right-wing politician Enoch Powell came to address a meeting of the Heraldic and Genealogical Society on the history of the House of Lords, his coming had to remain secret as police feared more riots. The practical results of the unrest were the staff/student meetings that were set up in the various faculties so that student views could be put forward. David attended these faculty events but found them quite tedious. Overall the unrest had damaged the public image of students and remains the main reason why David will still not take strike action.

Student life in Cambridge was markedly different in the late sixties from now. Sport was concentrated on the rugby and rowing clubs with cricket in the summer. Jogging was almost unheard of and no one attended a gym except for a few committed to training for major competitions. Rowing was a time-consuming job for those involved, with many students on the river before morning lectures. The future Olympic oarsman Chris Baillieu was reading history at Jesus in the year behind David and sought a little help from him when exam time came round. To gain a "blue" by being in the Cambridge boat for the annual boat race against Oxford was a full-time commitment. Very little football or soccer impinged on David's life. The vast majority of undergraduates rode bicycles to travel around the flat city and eventually David made a wobbly start on this art once he had a romantic interest in Girton College, one of the all-female colleges nearly three miles out of Cambridge up the very challenging Castle Hill. (See Family section!) Drugs were almost unnoticeable in daily life. One friend had been to a party where it was said there were some, but David was never offered any. A college bar which sold alcohol had just been opened when David arrived and there was often noise in the courtyards when the rowers and rugby players left. On one occasion a friend offered to buy David a lime juice in the bar and, knowing he was a teetotaler, had it made largely of vodka. David did not notice the difference! Drinking was much more confined to sportsmen in those days. Members of the college were expected to be in by 2 a.m. because technically receiving your degree still depended on your "pernoctation" record, the spending of the required number of nights in college, and not on the passing of examinations.

One of the main differences then was the purpose that brought students to the university. This was still a stage when many believed that the purpose of a university was to give a "liberal education." This policy resulted from a university committed to both teaching and research, believing that the one enriched the other. The emphasis was on the transmission of liberal and humane values and the development of personality and character. Commercial and monetary thinking with regard to higher education was only just starting. The historian E. P. Thompson published a book in 1971 called *Warwick University Limited* in which he denounced the trend to the commercialization of higher education. The book was widely applauded and there was an almost unanimous consensus of opinion that institutions of learning should not be run for commercial profit. Now, in 2014, every university in the United Kingdom is governed by profit-and-loss thinking, and higher education is part of the remit of the Department of Business, Innovation and Skills. Universities are now considered places simply to equip students for jobs so that they can earn more and pay more taxes. But if the record of the past is studied it is clear that many of the greatest scientific and philosophical discoveries took place almost by accident when brilliant minds were pursuing their own lines of enquiry and not when they were limited to closely defined areas with accountability to financial masters. The idea that universities were simply there to help get a job escalated in the years of Margaret Thatcher's leadership in the early 1980s and is now widespread in government thinking. David remains so grateful that this attitude did not prevail when he was an undergraduate.

In David's final year the question of the next step arose. He seriously considered law, his parents' mild preference, but he realized his love was for history. The choice then was either to do research if his results were good enough, or to apply to do a year's qualification for teaching history in schools. He was given a place to train as a teacher, but that did not become necessary. His first-class degree enabled him to follow the research route and so he became a postgraduate member of Jesus College and moved into a college flat in New Square (he married that summer—see later section!). After two years there he was elected a research fellow at Fitzwilliam College, Cambridge. These positions were given to scholars who showed promise in their particular academic discipline. The Elizabethan historian David Starkey, later a television star, had just finished one of these fellowships at Fitzwilliam and had moved to London, but returned from time to time to the college, where David used to meet him. A college room or study went with the job and free breakfasts, lunches, and dinners for three years.

Fitzwilliam College was in a much more recent building than Jesus. The college had started as Fitzwilliam House down in the city, opposite the Fitzwilliam Museum. It became a full college in the early 1960s and in 1967 opened its new building on the Huntingdon Road leading out of the city to the northwest. Life as a research student can be lonely, but once David was a fellow he thrived on the college life where he could mix with other fellows and their guests. David always loved the interaction with academics of other disciplines that dining in college gave him. If he was pursuing a topic, there would often be an expert in an adjacent field handy to consult. He would have breakfast and lunch there most days and dinner several times a week.

CHRISTIAN FAITH

Cambridge provided amazing opportunities for sampling a variety of Christian traditions. Town and gown offered rich resources for working out the relationship between the theological issues of the day. Used as he was to a busy Sunday, David found Cambridge Sundays even busier. First there was the Anglican communion in the college chapel at 8 a.m. followed by the chapel breakfast; at 10:45 there was morning worship at St. Andrew's Street Baptist Church, which was more traditional in style than his home church with a choir and more dignified music. The minister, the Reverend Arthur Jestice, was a kindly man who, in his preaching, related his message to various theologians such as Niebuhr and Barth. This excited David and the congregation welcomed him along with the many other students worshipping there. He was co-opted onto a committee to plan the church's 250th anniversary. Sunday lunchtimes were spent at a bread and cheese lunch with the college group of the Christian Union; after a gap of an hour or so, the tea meeting of the Robert Hall Society for Baptist students was held in the back hall of St. Andrew's Street church with tea at 4 p.m. and then a speaker; at 6:30 evening service would be at either at St. Andrew's Street or Zion Baptist Church across Parker's Piece; and at 8 p.m. there would either be the university sermon at Great St. Mary's Church in the city center, organized by the Reverend Hugh Montefiore, or the evangelistic sermon at Holy Trinity Church of England. Outstanding speakers visited these churches such as the first president of Zambia, Kenneth Kaunda, whose sermon on the transfiguration of Jesus David still remembers. The other sermons are duly recorded in his services notebook. Finally, when good Girton students had dutifully cycled the three miles back to college by their deadline of midnight and were safely in bed, Robert Hall Society members from the city colleges would meet for a late-night get-together.

The Cambridge Years

St. Andrew's Street Baptist Church, Cambridge

David was especially active in the college chapel community in his first year, attending the weekly discussion group and occasional late-evening compline services, as well as many evensongs. Elections to the chapel committee were contested on theological grounds, but David secured the most votes, being supported by the mainstream Anglicans in the chapel community, the evangelical members of the Christian Union and the Free Church contingent. He felt greatly honored to have been elected by such a varied constituency. Later he concentrated on the Robert Hall Society, named after a former distinguished Baptist minister in Cambridge, which proved very influential over him. It was designed for Baptist undergraduates from all the colleges and had the tea meeting with a speaker on the Sunday, small groups in the evening once a week, and WOW (War on Want) bread and cheese lunches one lunchtime. In the third year David became study secretary and wrote a series of Bible study outlines on Christian doctrine which, of course, he still possesses. In his third year he was vice president and made some lasting friendships in this group. Sadly the society no longer exists. It did provide several couples with their future partners for life and they have given years of service to Baptist and other churches throughout the country. It was also responsible for David becoming a visitor to Chinese restaurants. The atmospheric but somewhat down-market Hang Chow restaurant in Petty Cury in central Cambridge, later demolished for the Lion Yard development, became the venue for Robert Hall study groups' meals on special occasions and then he and his girlfriend started to visit themselves. Apart from the tasty food, Chinese restaurants are almost universally quick at serving customers, which greatly appeals to David.

Another area of Christian service where David was active in Cambridge was the local branch of the British and Foreign Bible Society, which aimed to distribute copies of the Bible or parts of it to as many people as possible. David had read the call from the then president of the Baptist Union of Great Britain and Ireland, the Reverend George Beasley-Murray, to spread the scriptures and so in the bath one day, in the depths of Jesus College, he conceived the idea of distributing a copy of John's gospel in modern English to the whole Cambridge undergraduate population, which numbered around ten thousand at that time. He raised the finance needed (£100) from interested individuals and recruited distributors for each college. He bought the gospels from the Bible Society and so it was natural for him to join their local committee. Interestingly his mother became secretary of the Nottingham Women's Bible Society group soon afterwards and was active for many years, helping place Bible story books in local schools. She had a special interest in the story of Mary Jones, the Welsh girl who had made a brave, difficult journey around 1800 to get a Bible. Always keen to do something with her hands, she made many Mary Jones dolls in Welsh costume which she sold for Bible Society funds.

In David's first term there was an exchange of views with Eamon Duffy, later the leading Roman Catholic historian of the Reformation in England. David thought, mistakenly, that Eamon could be persuaded to turn Protestant; Eamon responded by lending David a copy of Hans Küng's weighty treatise on *The Church*, which he duly read over the Christmas holiday. Eamon's friend, Sheridan Gilley, took David to various Roman Catholic and High Anglican events; other contacts took him to the Humanist Society; and he ventured to the Unitarian Chapel. It was a remarkably varied religious experience, but the core of it was supportively spiritual. During two of his terms David met for weekly prayer with his fellow student John Howes. This was the start of a practice that he still continues today with two or three others from his local church. In all these ways David's Christian faith deepened.

HISTORY

The history course in the first two years consisted of a weekly essay which was handed in to a supervisor before supervisions and was the subject of an hour's discussion. Supervisions were one-to-one. Although this does not sound too demanding, undergraduates were expected to read a vast number of books for each essay, extract the main argument and blend each one into their own essays. This is a skill that has proved most useful over the years. One of the things David likes to do most is to spend a day "gutting" two or three dozen books and then evaluating their contents in his own work. The university history course offered, among other options, medieval European and early modern English history, "early modern" meaning from the fifteenth to the eighteenth centuries. The teaching was organized in college as far as possible and Jesus had some outstanding young PhD students to teach him. In the summer term of his first year David chose as an option the History of Political Thought, taught by a young left-wing research student, John Barber, who went on to be fellow in politics and lay dean at King's College. This option proved extremely significant, giving David an awakening to the history of ideas in general. He still teaches a course on the History of Political Thought today. Supervisors varied and in second year some of the courses were poorly taught. But in the Lent term of 1970, in his second year, he had individual sessions with Moses Finley, later Sir Moses, who was a brilliant supervisor of Ancient History. He was willing to double the length of time of a supervision just to carry on discussing historical issues. As it was the fourth or fifth time David had studied the Greek and Roman world, he was comfortable with the basic characters and events and was able to become involved in discussing wider issues. Moses Finley, a Jewish American fugitive from McCarthyism in the United States, had been given refuge at Jesus College by the master, Sir Denys Page. International events therefore had had a direct influence on his being there to teach David at this critical point in his degree. Finley was not always popular with classicists because of his examining broad themes, not texts, but for David this dimension was exciting. He always remembers the phone call coming during one of his supervisions offering Finley the University Chair of Ancient History. Finley was a great encouragement to David, who at school had written extremely long essays, almost of the "write everything you know about..." type. He had not been used to producing a tightly argued case by drawing on the evidence in the sources. Now he was able to debate the different sides of an issue and to come down on which was the more convincing. He was refining his technique by being encouraged to discern fresh patterns in the past. David's mother long wanted him to become a lawyer. In a way he has, but as a history "lawyer," arguing his cases in print.

Each undergraduate in a college had a director of studies. The Jesus College director of studies for history was Vivian Fisher and before Tripos Part 1 he encouraged David to write a full three-hour exam paper once a week before the actual exams in order to reduce the stress of the events themselves and to help him learn to marshal his thoughts more quickly. He understood David very well and David feels a great debt to him. He still encourages this technique at Stirling and many students have felt the benefit. Without this he would probably not have obtained a first-class grade in Part 1. He continued to have some excellent teaching. In Part 2 in his third year David was taken by Richard Tuck as his first supervisee on Religion and Ideas in England, 1500 to 1650, which again was on the history of ideas. Richard was a year ahead at the college and had already been helpful in lending David some of his essays to read. This showed David even more of what could be done in arguing a case. Richard went on to be Professor of Government at Harvard. In the Lent term 1971 David took Theories of the Modern State, again with John Barber, and throughout the year he chose Edward Norman's special subject of the Irish Party under Parnell in the 1880s which was to provide good background for his future studies of the British prime minister, William Gladstone. Edward Norman, a specialist in Victorian issues of church and state, took over as director of studies for David's final year.

The Cambridge system included two voluntary lectures a week specifically on your course as well as a range of others. These lectures took place for history students on the newly opened Sidgwick Site, on the other side of town from David's college. There too was the new famous/infamous, award-winning Seeley History Library that had opened in 1968 and became loved and hated in equal measure. Spectacular in its architecture, it could be very hot or very cold and pieces fell off it from time to time! Lectures were not compulsory, and David was selective, but he also took advantage of hearing many of the great names of the History Faculty, not all of whom proved interesting. He enjoyed Michael Crawford's classical lectures and Duncan Forbes on Theories of the Modern State in his final year. A highlight was listening to Quentin Skinner's first ever lecture series on the history of political thought. Skinner went on to be Professor of Political Science at Cambridge and then Regius Professor of Modern History and changed the whole methodology in this field, becoming known as the founder of the "Cambridge School" of thinkers in this area. It was with some satisfaction that David was asked to speak at a conference assessing the value of Skinner's methods for the history of religious ideas held in Cambridge in 2004. (David prepared an evaluation of the Thursday and Friday conference proceedings early on the Saturday morning, a paper which is now in print.) He did not limit himself to just history lectures. He greatly enjoyed David Newsome's series of lectures in the Divinity Faculty on nineteenth-century church history and sampled many others there.

His favorite library for research was—and remains—the Cambridge University Library in West Road. In this copyright library where every book published in the United Kingdom must be deposited, many books are on open shelves and it is possible to pursue a single topic to one's heart's content. In many fields there is no waiting for books to be brought to you. Often David has tried to do speedy research in other libraries, only to find it will take longer to fetch the books for him than the time he has available. At the British Library in London books were often said to have been lost in the blitz of the Second World War and were unavailable. Not so at the Cambridge UL.

During his first two terms David was so immersed in a variety of activities that his essays, though rarely neglected, lacked depth. That began to change, but he had little idea of how well he could do in the university examinations at the end of his second year. When the results appeared he looked first at the 2:1 list, then at the 2:2 list and only then at the firsts—where he found his name. He then realized that the news was on the front page of the *Times* because the Prince of Wales was taking the same exams! He also obtained a first in the examinations at the end of the third year.

Once he had started teaching undergraduates (see later section), he joined the Young Historians' Group for teaching members of the History Faculty under the age of forty. These were heady days for this group which included some of the leading historians of the next generation: Simon Schama, David Abulafia, and David Cannadine among others. When he was secretary, David had the unenviable task of removing members once they reached forty!

The most atmospheric event he attended was the seminar run by George Kitson Clark, a Reader in British Constitutional History, in the Great Gatehouse of Trinity College. He had attended one when still an undergraduate before receiving a polite note that it was strictly for postgraduates. The meetings started at 8:30 p.m. with sherry for those who wanted it. A speaker would start at 9 p.m. and finish at 9:50 and then there would be lengthy discussion. Kitson Clark himself would often come in with a devastating comment, puncturing arguments at a blow. When one speaker had read a paper pointing out the surprising number of weighty people who believed in the appearance of the angel of Mons to encourage British troops in that First World War engagement, Kitson Clark observed that he had known most of the people cited and they could not possibly have believed in the angel! The whole atmosphere of this evening was something that David savored.

When it came to choosing a topic to research for a doctor of philosophy, David knew that he wanted to work in the area of Nonconformists and politics. This choice was because he had been gathering material ready for a history of his church in Nottingham and realized there was no good book on Nonconformity and politics at the start of the twentieth century. He was actually registered officially to study the economics of chapel building and is profoundly grateful he never did that. He was assigned to David Thompson of Fitzwilliam College as a supervisor who reassured him that he could change topics and so David set off on his area of interest. He had trips to various collections of manuscripts. For example he visited the headquarters of the Chubb Lock and Safe Company in London and was caught up in a bomb threat connected with the troubles in Northern Ireland which was never reported in the press. David and I both studied the letters of Lord Rosebery in the National Library of Scotland. There were no accessible photocopiers in those days, and so I wrote out the relevant passages he wanted. I was very grateful when photocopiers did appear! When he visited the National Library of Wales in Aberystwyth, he had his first experience of Welsh nationalism and the depth of feeling around the preservation of the Welsh language. His research gave opportunities for trips.

My father played a crucial part in the completion of the PhD which has resulted in benefit to several generations of David's students. As a civil engineer, he was used to setting time scales and deadlines for tasks to be completed and so he asked David for his timetable of work and required regular updates. This proved invaluable for the PhD and later for book writing. So many historians go on and on researching for their books which they believe will convey the absolutely accurate and up-to-date state of the subject, but David soon realized that it was better to produce something within a reasonable time limit rather than wait for years until nothing comes of the research. David also found, as he has done ever since, that it is in the process of writing up the research that understanding comes. He still recommends something like his father-in-law's technique to his research students.

In 1974 he took a term off PhD research to write an essay for the university Hulsean Prize which he submitted at Christmas 1974 on "The Dissenting Idea of a University." He was awarded the prize, which was good considering he had finished it around 3 a.m. on the morning of the deadline. The actual writing for the PhD was done in a very short time. It was written between the start of August and the end of September 1975. Two weeks were taken out for a holiday in Inverness and in those days the manuscript had to be prepared by somebody else. David's typist lived miles out in the Fens although she worked in Cambridge. Things became frantic getting the corrected proofs to her and at one stage we had the sheets, the top ones and the carbon copies, all over our living room floor. Nowadays on computers students can go on and on correcting the text until the last minute. It was not a bad thing that a whistle had to be blown and the text given to the typist. Things moved quickly in those days. The viva was called only two weeks later in Queen's College, Oxford, where Kenneth Morgan (now Lord) and Peter Clarke were the examiners. This completed the study for the PhD and David's mother, who had missed his original graduation, was able to attend the degree ceremony.

FAMILY

What changes did Cambridge bring about in family life? David had never been interested in girlfriends. He had had so many absorbing interests in Nottingham and had worked so hard that they had not come into his thinking. He had had brief contact with girls from Nottingham Girls' High School and at church but only when organization required. When he went up to Cambridge in 1968 the ratio of male undergraduates to female was 11:1 with no mixed colleges and only three all-female colleges: Newnham,

Girton, and New Hall. This was amazingly different from the present position where there are roughly half men and half women. It was not likely that David statistically would find a girlfriend while at Cambridge. But that was reckoning without the Robert Hall Society where Baptist students met. Female numbers were increased by trainee teachers from Homerton College and nurses from Addenbrooke's Hospital. I had already spent one year at Girton College, built at a safe three-mile distance from the center so that the early students in the 1860s would not be distracted by men! I was well integrated into the society and went to the after-church meeting to welcome freshers at the Reverend Arthur Jestice's home on the Sunday evening before term started in early October 1968. David was there but gave the impression of being a confident returner, not an anxious fresher, and so I went looking for the more nervous of them to talk to. I did not speak to him that evening. We both attended Robert Hall meetings and I kept hearing things about this newcomer and how he liked books and discussion, and so my interest was aroused, for I had decided that if I was to marry it was to be to someone I would not be bored with! (I think that is one aim in life that I have definitely achieved!) At the very end of the first term, just before Christmas, I was very happy to meet David as I came out of Mowbray's, the religious bookseller then on King's Parade, especially as I had bought a selection of books as Christmas gifts including a life of William Booth (the founder of the Salvation Army who came from Nottingham!) and the story of the medieval scholar Peter Abelard. We had a brief conversation about the books and I felt I held my own well. I was at Girton College reading classics, which consisted of Latin, Greek, and ancient history, and had done A level history at school so that I knew the area we were talking about.

Early the next term there was to be a debate at the Robert Hall Society about Sunday observance and David and I were to speak on the stricter side of the question. And so at the start of the Lent Term in January we met in his room and I sampled his mother's amazing cakes for the first time. I learned you had to be careful accepting coffee from him. David was taught not to waste food and so he used to keep his small daily milk bottles (delivered to his room) well past their use-by date! I never suffered ill effects but my mother did and so the story of David poisoning his future mother-in-law became legendary! The first time he actually asked me out was to hear Dr. Martyn Lloyd-Jones, who was speaking in one of the churches. I thought it might have been the two of us and wondered if this was intentional on his part, but then someone else joined us so I was not at all sure. One evening two groups of Robert Hall members met at a Chinese restaurant and David mentioned to the group that he had two tickets for Bach's Mass in B Minor. Someone jumped at the offer to go with him and I felt a bit confused about why he had not asked me. Apparently he was hoping I would volunteer. David used to walk back from the Sidgwick Site to the center talking to me before I set off up the Castle Hill and the three-mile cycle ride back to college. I always assumed he was staying in town. Only much later did I discover that he turned round and walked straight back to where we had come from. He was really trying to get to know me. At this stage no one knew that we were interested in each other apart from one or two of my closest friends. Girton College was celebrating its one hundredth anniversary that March and there was a Centenary Ball. My friend Celia Hammond (now Fox) knew I liked David so she told him that I was sad not to be going. To his eternal credit he asked me to go. Balls are not David's natural habitat but there we sat listening to steel bands and Manfred Mann's live music until he left for college on the bus provided at 3 a.m. He had of course brought a useful book to read on the way home! By the Easter vacation we decided that he would come over from Nottingham with his parents, officially for a day's sightseeing in my hometown of Northampton, some sixty miles from Nottingham, also in the East Midlands.

I had been brought up in Northampton although my parents came from Bournemouth. I had an elder brother Michael who had married his fiancée Sheila a few days before I first met David. They went on to have a son and a daughter, Katharine and Jonathan, and so David eventually acquired a niece and nephew. Northampton was a strong Nonconformist area with Philip Doddridge's academy of the early eighteenth century one of its claims to fame, and with many, many businesses, especially boot and shoe firms, run by Nonconformists or Free Churchmen. My parents came from a long line of Congregationalists, one of the largest Nonconformist denominations, having met at the East Cliff Church in Bournemouth. When David started working on the PhD we actually had links to almost all the relevant denominations between our two families. My father was a civil engineer, working with a local firm, Kottler and Heron, specializing in roads, bridges, and water purification. He preached regularly in village churches and was a deacon and Boy Scout master in our own church, Abington Avenue Congregational. My mother had taken an external London University degree through Southampton University College in Latin, French, and history in the mid-1930s and had taught briefly before she was married in December

1939. Married women were not allowed to teach at that time and anyway in the war my parents had to move a great deal as my father built emergency airfields before being called up into the army and being involved in producing part of the top-secret Mulberry Harbour that was so crucial in the D-Day landings of 1944. In Northampton my mother was active in the Free Church Women's Council (a pan-Nonconformist organization) and became its national president in 1968/69. This entailed speaking around the country on religious and social issues involving the churches. We had all worshipped at Abington Avenue Congregational Church, but I had started attending Broadmead Baptist Church shortly before I went up to Girton in 1967. The minister there had told me about the Robert Hall Society and that is how I became involved so quickly. I had made my own Christian commitment shortly before leaving school (I attended Northampton High School for Girls from 1953 until 1966) and was baptized in my first year in Cambridge at Zion Baptist Church there.

And so the visit to Northampton took place. In April 1969 David's parents drove him over and I succumbed to a nonstop few hours of thorough visiting of Northampton's historic sites, and, believe me, there are plenty of them! His parents went round too and his mother was so relieved when half way through my mother said she wanted a cup of tea! But I ploughed bravely on. (David has always been keen to see any place as thoroughly as he can. I very quickly learned to limit my sightseeing with him. These days when he is in a new town or secondhand bookshop, I find either a new book or a coffee shop and do the crossword. I do not feel deprived. I enjoy the space!) Back in Cambridge in the summer term we spent more time together. Talking was the key. We loved conversation with each other and like it even more now, well over forty years later. We kept our friendship private for several months as we grew to know each other but that was quite a slow process. David has never taken regular coffee or tea breaks. The University Library had an excellent tea room, but I never persuaded David to join me there except at lunchtime!

That summer was my twenty-first birthday, on July 2, and our friendship was public by then. David came over for a party in the garden at my house. In the autumn he brought his father's old wartime bicycle back complete with black-out paint over the front lamp and learned to ride it for the first time. He was not a natural cyclist. On one occasion he arrived at a bread and cheese lunch with holes in his trousers and bloodstained knees. His parents had always maintained that David had poor coordination and had discouraged him from trying to cycle. We came to know each other better in his second year when I was president of the Robert Hall Society and in my final year. We wrote to each other every day when not at Cambridge and these letters still exist. In David's third year I was doing a one-year teaching qualification at Hughes Hall, still in Cambridge, and we became engaged one wet November Saturday in Newmarket. Each autumn we would have an afternoon trip out on a bus (few students had cars in those days) and we had spent a pleasant time in the shops and at the Congregational church's sale of work. Just as the return bus was coming he asked me to do him the honor of becoming my wife. I always joked and said I said yes so that I did not miss the bus! We had an engagement party in the Prioress' Room at the college and planned the wedding for July 31, 1971. From January until Easter in 1970 I stayed in Sydenham, South London, on teaching practice, but we still met at weekends when we could. These few months were marred by Bill's lung cancer becoming worse and sadly he died the day before David's finals started. Shortly after the funeral his mother was taken to hospital with a suspected heart attack and it was uncertain if the wedding could go ahead. We had no idea if David would be doing research for a PhD by then or if he was to have a lifetime of school teaching ahead of him. We have always thought that if he had found the right school he would have been a conscientious and committed history teacher, willing to run out-of-school activities.

The wedding took place as planned and Vera managed to attend the day. The service was held at Broadmead Baptist Church, Northampton, where I had been worshipping since the sixth form. The Reverend Roger Hayden married us and was clever in his sensitive preparation and sound advice. He remains a wise mentor. The reception was held at Abington Avenue Congregational Church, where I had grown up, and after the meal we adjourned to our family home at 7 Weston Way, where we had a marquee on the lawn and chairs and tables in the sun for afternoon tea. As we had no car, we left from Rugby by train for two weeks at a wonderful bed and breakfast in Windermere, recommended to us by the equally wonderful church secretary of Zion Baptist Church, Sidney Charge. Run by a Mrs. Wragg, the establishment provided enough cooked breakfast to live on for the whole day. Mrs. Wragg was keen for us to write in her visitors' book at the end. David wrote:

> Want a boon on your honeymoon? Pack your bags and come to Wraggs!

David really should have found a job writing verses for greetings cards. He can produce verse of that type at the drop of a hat. He also takes on the flavor of whatever he is reading. This can be tricky if he is reading the elaborate style of Gladstone, the Victorian prime minister, for several weeks. He has to be careful going into shops not to scare the assistants by asking in nineteenth-century prose! Book collecting was well under way by then. One day during the honeymoon we caught the bus to Kendal, went to a bookshop that had twenty-three rooms and bought forty-seven books which we then took back on the bus to Windermere. How did we transport them to Cambridge? Well, those were the wonderful days of Passenger Luggage in Advance on the railways and so we could send them home to meet us there.

David and Eileen's wedding, 1971. From left to right: The Reverend Roger Hayden, Margaret Lacey, Sheila and Mike Lacey, David and Eileen, David Lacey, Vera Bebbington, Clarice Urquhart

We rented from Jesus College the two upstairs floors of a house at 1 New Square in Cambridge. New Square was an 1820s housing development which at that time looked on to a car park which has now been put down to grass. As we were on the end, the rooms were wedge shaped, which meant that they were hard to carpet. The end living room looked straight across the grass of Christ's Pieces and was a wonderful position for our first Christmas tree. The house certainly had character. Bath water was heated by an enormous gas-fired cylinder that we lit and which then exploded into life.

One day when we spilt a bottle of milk in the kitchen, the liquid completely disappeared. We found it all in the kitchen of the old lady downstairs. Fortunately by this time she was in care because she had taken to coming up at various times of day or night to ask what day it was. On the second (third in American terms) floor there were two tiny bedrooms. In the built-in cupboard of one of them we found newspaper from the early 1820s stuck on as wall paper. As a civil engineer my father was always very concerned about the weight of books that David kept up in these rooms, but despite his gloomy predictions and load-bearing calculations, the house never did fall down! There was a small yard at the back, but to reach that I had to go out of the front door with all my washing, right round the property and in at the back gate. I had a full-time post at the Perse School for Girls teaching classics. We were never very clever house tenants. We bought a piano quite cheaply one night because I missed playing, only to find it would not fit up the narrow winding stairs. It lived in a coal house for a while and then we had to pay to have the end window taken out and the piano lifted through with a crane. Within a year we were moving and so out it had to come again! Our cheap piano had become very costly, but we did give great amusement to passersby.

1 New Square, Cambridge, seen from Christ's Pieces

One or two school friends from Nottingham helped us with the flat. Richard Kidd helped paint it in return for a potted course in the history of philosophy from David. Richard had made a Christian commitment with

David soon after arriving at Cambridge and was on the way to ordination as a Baptist minister and later became principal of the Northern Baptist College and then co-principal of the Northern Baptist Learning Community. We developed a very close connection with Richard, as we did with Rosemary Margetson who lived above me at Hughes Hall, where we were both training to teach. They met first at our engagement party and then at our wedding. They contacted each other after this event, married a few months later and had four lovely children. We became guardians to all four and often planned how we would manage if anything happened to the parents.

When David was awarded a research fellowship at Fitzwilliam College in 1973, we needed to move out of the Jesus College flat. Thanks to help from my parents and David's mother, who had just received a little money from the sale of David's grandmother's home, we were able to buy our first house, 69 Richmond Road, conveniently situated just off the Huntingdon Road, just beyond the college. With one large living room and a large kitchen downstairs and three bedrooms and a bathroom upstairs, this end-of-terrace, pale-brick house suited us really well. It had a tiny garden in the front and a larger one at the back. We had a party-line telephone which we shared with a house further along the road which meant that if the people at the other house were using the phone you had to wait until they finished. It also meant you could hear their conversation, but that was not "done." I cycled to work every morning down into Cambridge and David went off to college breakfast and the day's research.

The Cambridge Years

69 Richmond Road, Cambridge

Richmond Road was an excellent place to live. It was unnerving in the first couple of years when a serial rapist was on the loose in the city. I always remember that our neighbors knew the identity of the rapist long before the police caught him. The husband worked with this man and it was well known that he could squeeze through the tiniest open window. We had joined Zion Baptist Church as members in 1971. I had been baptized there by the Reverend W. G. Channon in my first year and we became members. As it was so close to New Square, we always seemed to arrive late. Once we were in Richmond Road and had to cycle for twenty minutes to reach the church, we were usually on time. Soon my mother needed to change her car to an automatic and we inherited her pale blue Morris Minor. We loved that car. David learned to drive on it, taught on three occasions by my father and then by me! He was not a natural at steering but with enough practice passed his test at the second attempt. Once we had that vehicle we could travel further afield on trips and it had the most amazing capacity for carrying secondhand books.

A significant development took place at Richmond Road in David's musical appreciation. He had enjoyed singing in the school choir, but most of the music at his house on records had been from the Romantic period and left him unmoved. One Saturday morning I heard a concert on Radio Three, the BBC's classical music station, of David Munro playing some early music from the sixteenth to the eighteenth centuries on early instruments in a concert for children. I knew at once that David would find this sort of music exciting and we started to collect David Munro's records. We could also attend concerts, at King's College for instance, where baroque music was played from time to time. Early music was then looked down on as primitive by many classical musicians and few people cared about the authentic sound that the early instruments would have made. Now it is mainstream and whole orchestras strive to recreate the original sounds. When pressed, David will admit that he likes music written only before 1750 and he has an extensive collection of early music compact discs ready to play in his library. This taste can cause problems for him in worship services with a contemporary style of music.

Permanent jobs were few and far between and there was no guarantee of a post at the end of the PhD. But a history lectureship came up at the University of Stirling and so David applied, was interviewed on April 1, 1976, and was appointed to the job. I was a little apprehensive about moving so far north but David told me that a brand new shopping center was being built and the Thistle Centre remains an excellent place today. My parents had moved to the south coast in 1971 after the wedding and my father had a pre-retirement job there. My mother never really recovered from my moving so far away. This was the start of our north/south journeys to pay visits to both families at Christmas, at Easter, and in the summer until Vera's death in 1997, just after my father's, and my mother's death in 2008.

TEACHING AND PREACHING

Many of the patterns of David's life, the study of history and the exploration of the Christian faith, developed in Cambridge. A major new one began because he started to teach and preach regularly. Teaching at Cambridge was organized in a fairly fluid way, with colleges seeking supervisors for their students from elsewhere if they had nobody suitable. In the second year of research, while still at Jesus, David was asked to supervise the new history of education unit for various colleges. This arrangement was made because the man in charge of this subject remembered him from his application to do teacher training and so when supervisors were needed he was an obvious candidate. If you had not taken a course in a subject, you were expected to be able to master it and teach it with the skills you had learned. David drew up a booklist for the subject (being mistaken by the Education Faculty librarian as a student in the process), which became the standard course bibliography a year or two later. In his first year at Fitzwilliam he taught modern British history, the next year Religion and Society since 1770, and by the third year there he was teaching for thirteen colleges. All the students came as individuals or in pairs. Seminar teaching for undergraduates was a thing of the future for him.

While at Fitzwilliam from 1973 to 1976 David enjoyed being part of the history teaching team under Lesley Wayper. He was responsible each year for examining candidates for admission to the college and taught Theories of the Modern State to its undergraduates. Lesley recruited him one year to give a lecture to trainee army officers on the idea of authority, a taxing commission from which he probably learned more than they. During this time he was a regular attender at modern history seminars. He enjoyed the informality of one regularly held at Newnham College by Gillian Sutherland, a historian of education, who became one of David's referees. Because the "powers that be" in the history faculty saw this group as a radical alternative to the Kitson Clark seminar and David became its secretary, he felt branded as a subversive influence in some quarters. He, on the contrary, saw the two bodies as complementary. Meanwhile, as a research fellow, he was qualified to deliver an annual series of lectures in the History Faculty. Choosing the subject "Political Dissent," he spent half the lectures critiquing the influential hypothesis of the left-wing historian E. P. Thompson that Methodism was a dysfunctional symptom of the oppression of the working class. He was still making out that case forty-five years later.

A Patterned Life

Fitzwilliam College, Cambridge

In 1971 Cambridgeshire Baptist Association consisted of forty-one chapels, many of which had no minister and a very few members. It became known at Zion that David had preached a little and so, joining the Local Preachers' Association, he was let loose on the chapels. When a mentor went with him to hear a test sermon, David remembers with embarrassment that he told the few people in the tiny chapel at Prickwillow, way out in the Fens, well below sea level, what the book of Job was *not* about. The mentor kindly pointed out that it could have been more helpful to say what it was about! Fortunately that chapel is still open and serves as the main worship center for the village. But the chapel people were unfailingly kind, hospitable, and encouraging and gradually his skills were honed. We still have these sermons, written in David's own shorthand. I feel sad that many of them were preached to only four or five people. I have always felt they deserved a wider audience. (For an example of a recent sermon, see appendix 3.) David has always tried to preach closely from a Bible passage using fresh thoughts each time. I have found his Old Testament ones particularly good. He takes a passage which seems to offer a very unlikely basis for a sermon and turns it into spiritually helpful material. Another occasion we remember is when we were due in the town of March, some twenty-five miles from home. We left after the right time in the first place and then became stuck behind a cycling race. On the fen roads it is often difficult to overtake and we arrived very late. The poor church secretary was anxiously scanning up and down the road while someone else had started the service.

The Cambridge Years

Once again we were graciously received and learned a useful lesson about leaving enough time to reach our destinations.

One interesting spin-off from the preaching was that David's lecturing style was being fashioned by preaching far more than by experience of delivering lectures. I was his sternest critic and would mention excessive hand waving or other gestures. I expected him to speak clearly, smile at his audience, and make the content interesting with plenty of relevant illustrations, often from his historical research. This early practice in public speaking established a paradigm. It remains the basis of his academic lecturing method today and people all over the world have appreciated his style which was developed due to the tolerance of the wonderful Fen people in their tiny chapels.

TRIPS AND TRAVEL

Although Cambridge was only sixty miles or so from Nottingham, the route was cross country and so as an undergraduate David felt remote from home during term time. Once we had become friends, each of us spent a great deal of time traveling in coaches up and down the M1 motorway between our homes or on trains to and from Nottingham. The summer of 1969 was a busy one. David stayed with his friend Michel Hunter in South Harting in West Sussex where his father was rector and also went to Minehead in north Somerset for two weeks with his parents with the usual intense round of historic sites and bookshops. He also stayed in Norwich with Gordon Waller, his school friend who enjoyed visiting parish churches. David remembers that on the last day they could not decide which to do, parish churches or bookshops. Gordon was keener on the former and by now David was on the latter. And so they agreed to work separately that day. It was during that stay that David ventured into poetry for the first time. The river in Nottingham is called the Leen and so the poem was all about Eileen and the Leen. Unfortunately I was not over enthusiastic in my response because I was on a very stormy sailing holiday with my parents (the only time I allowed myself to be talked into going on one!) and I was more concerned about staying upright than poems. That was David's last attempt at poetry, at least where I am concerned. We still have the letter with the poem.

New patterns of travel could develop once we were married. Before we had the car, our trips were by bus or train. In 1972 we visited Bath for the wedding of our friends from the Robert Hall Society, Robin and Rosemary

Bolton. Bath just happened to have twelve bookshops at the time! Once we had the car available we were able to travel further afield and spent the first of many holidays in the West Country. We were based in Bideford in North Devon and well remember our ignorance of how to stop when driving down steep hills. Cambridge presents very few opportunities for this skill and we had some dangerous moments until we mastered how to brake on and off, rather than have brakes full on with the ensuing smell of burning brake pads! In 1975 we drove all the way to Inverness, some five hundred miles, sharing the driving, and visited some of the Urquhart family sites for the first time, including Urquhart Castle on Loch Ness and the Black Isle. When David was offered a job in Stirling the following year we were aware of how far south it is in Scotland, having been touring the Highlands the year before. I drove all the way home from Inverness to Cambridge in a single day on roads that were very different from now because David had cricked his neck in a very rare game of tennis with me!

It was during these years that we developed our love for British bed and breakfast establishments. They are very different from US ones. They give basic hospitality in a private house, usually with a "Great British Breakfast" of bacon, egg, fried bread, and so on. Both of us had been used to holidaying in small hotels with our families, but now we preferred these places to stay that are rather looked down on by many. We have had some wonderful experiences. In Bideford, for example, we stayed at the same time as a man who worked for Heinz as a "spag(hetti) man" and kept us entertained with stories of how the canning process can go wrong. Inverness was the most memorable. We eventually worked out that the landlady made her husband sleep in the airing cupboard where the clean linen was kept. They had fallen out many years before about treatment for their terminally ill son and had not spoken since. Her father had been station manager at Ballater station near Balmoral, the royal home in the Highlands, and so had welcomed many royals on to the platform. She kept his boots, beautifully polished and full of bright red geraniums, by her front door. Also staying was a couple. The husband rarely spoke to his wife at all during breakfasts but would examine railway timetables instead. He would occasionally read her something about a train. Apart from the experiences, David always loves discovering local color from the owners: advice on things to see and do and information about the ethos of an area. Our favorite bed and breakfast was in York where our host went in for malapropisms. He suggested we visit a local "naturist" reserve to look at the wildlife! But they were kindness itself.

His only regret was he had to go to work on the Saturday we were leaving and therefore could not see David loading up the accumulation of boxes of books we had acquired into our Morris Minor. He could never understand why we were going to places such as Halifax and Huddersfield while most visitors would go off to enjoy the lovely Yorkshire Dales. The reason was, of course, the bookshops. David has an uncanny knack of always being able to load the books into whatever space is available! To this day David would prefer a bed and breakfast to any hotel. These days they are far more regulated and required to have minimum standards, but they still provide excellent value for money.

BOOKS AND BOOK COLLECTING

Cambridge provided many opportunities for book experiences. Apart from the two libraries already mentioned, there was the Classics Faculty Library, then in Mill Lane. This became even more attractive when a certain Girtonian was also studying there. There was also a selection of really good secondhand bookshops. One of them, David's, which still survives in the city center in St. Edward's Passage, used to have a market stall as well as the shop. On a Saturday morning before working, David would go, along with other enthusiasts, to sift through the new stock as it was put out in the open air. He went up to Cambridge with a well-established bibliophile reputation. When the student newspaper needed an article on the local secondhand bookshops, an old boy of his school asked David to write it. In his first year the old branch of Heffer's bookshop was in its original home in Petty Cury, where Lion Yard now stands. That had a large quantity of secondhand stock. So did Galloway and Porter in Sidney Street and in another shop David bought the six-volume set of the works of the Baptist minister at the turn of the nineteenth century, Robert Hall, for £1.50.

When David traveled elsewhere he relied on public transport and taking books home could be a challenge. He remembers coming back from south London once with an enormous box that he had to persuade a friend to help him with in order to get it back home. On a visit to Oxford in 1969, in the Turl Cash Bookshop, alas no longer there, he bought six biographies of Congregational ministers from the library of Mansfield College that they were selling off. When seeing that he had bought six, the proprietor offered him any more that he wanted for one shilling (5p) each and so David bought fifty-nine books there that day. That remains the record for purchases on a single occasion from one shop. Unfortunately he could not carry them all back to Regent's Park College where he was staying and so he had to leave some in the porch of St. Mary Magdalene Church hoping that they would enjoy sanctuary there until he could fetch them. They did.

When he was living in Nottingham his parents were already raising eyebrows at the volume of books in his bedroom. I can never claim that I did not know what I was letting myself in for. Book collecting became David's chief and most absorbing hobby. Whenever in a strange town he would seek out the secondhand book dealers and it was a regular pattern after a trip for him to dust, sort, and shelve his new acquisitions. The collection gradually grew.

POLITICS

David had not taken a deep interest in politics in Nottingham, but had absorbed the conventional Conservatism of the family. He discovered, however, through the history of Queensberry Street that Nonconformists had been solidly Liberal and so by the time he graduated he had turned into a natural Liberal. The Nonconformists whom he studied for his PhD made a hero of William Ewart Gladstone, the Liberal prime minister of the later years of Victoria's reign. Unfortunately, some canvassers for the Liberal Party in the early seventies called at our door and stressed how keen the party was to move away from its old-fashioned values and become a party of the modern day. The more they spoke the more they alienated one of their potential voters! When later David wrote his first small book on Mr. Gladstone he tried to show how a man with conservative theology was perfectly able to be a liberal in politics. It was in Cambridge that he became increasingly interested in the relation of religion and politics. He became heavily involved in the Shaftesbury Project, a venture springing from the Inter-Varsity Fellowship that encouraged working out the social and political implications of evangelical faith. He was duly invited to write a brief account of Lord Shaftesbury, the man after whom it was named, and incurred the wrath of some readers for daring to point out that he was unpleasant to Gladstone.

SUMMARY

In the Cambridge years David's faith deepened, his book collecting broadened, and he visited many parts of the United Kingdom. The three most significant developments were in his family life, his historical and political thinking and his preaching and teaching. Chinese restaurants had also started to feature. The groundwork was being laid and strengthened for the career he has pursued over the subsequent nearly four decades in Stirling and around the world.

3

The Stirling Years

THE FAMILY

The move north took place in July 1976 to our present home, 5 Pullar Avenue, Bridge of Allan. Although I had been up to see the area, I did not view the house before we agreed to buy. We decided it was easier to move in and then change later if we were not happy rather than my taking time off teaching to travel the four hundred miles just to view. Having a house already, we knew roughly what we were looking for and I felt I could trust David to make a good decision. That was slightly tested by the gloomy aspect of the building when we first arrived one evening at dusk after the long drive up, but I quickly felt better in the sun next morning and we have been delighted with our purchase ever since. We had to rebuild the back part in 2006 when we added an extra bedroom, but otherwise it remains very much the same as when we bought it. Bridge of Allan remains a pleasant, small town of some eight thousand residents three miles from Stirling and next door to the university with excellent communications in most directions. The motorway connections have always been good, but nowadays it is possible to join the M9 motorway just over two miles from the house and remain on a motorway or dual carriageway to the south coast of England, some five hundred miles away.

The Stirling Years

5 Pullar Avenue, Bridge of Allan

We were very fortunate to have a ready-made community to join at Stirling Baptist Church where we had worshiped on our visit up to see the area; David attended the mid-week meeting on the day of his job interview. We had already met the minister and his wife, James and Helen Taylor, and we were to receive many kindnesses from them over the next forty years. The church at that time met on a site where McDonald's restaurant now is in Murray Place in Stirling city center. At that time Stirling consisted of some sixty thousand residents. For well over a thousand years there has been a town on the site next to the last crossing point of the River Forth before it widens out to the sea. A castle had been built in the Middle Ages to defend the river crossing and many battles took place near this strategic location. Stirling had become a flourishing county town. In the 1960s it was the seat of local government and gained a new university.

We gradually came to know the surrounding area as well as Edinburgh and Glasgow, forty and thirty miles away respectively. We did not have much money left after buying the house and so it was exciting a year or so later to visit Paris to stay with my brother's family. I took a while to find a job but eventually started teaching part-time at a local secondary school. Over the next six years I taught Latin, Greek, classical studies, and religious education at three local secondary schools and also qualified to teach English. I taught part-time because it was thought more conducive to having a baby but no baby appeared after several years. Some friends who had adopted locally happened to tell us that the adoption list was opening for one twenty-four hour period in the near future and if we did not apply we might not have another chance. The supply of babies was disappearing because of changing social attitudes and the contraceptive pill. And so we applied along with hundreds of others and, much to our surprise, we were selected for assessment. There was a long wait for this process; eventually it was spread out over a series of months and after many visits and discussions with the local social work department we were passed as suitable parents—by this stage they were adamant that they were looking for parents for children and not the other way round. And so, at last, on November 5, 1984, Guy Fawkes Night in the United Kingdom, with bonfires and fireworks all around, we were taken to see a beautiful baby girl. We had two days to make up our mind but the decision did not take long. We collected Anne, as we called her, on November 7 and brought her home. I had had to leave work on the previous Friday, which was quite strange because we had not seen the baby at that point. There was no question of maternity leave, but, on the contrary, we were taken aback when my employers decided I had been overpaid and asked for several hundred pounds of money back! Anne settled in amazingly well with good sleep patterns. She was eleven weeks old when we had her and I found that a very comfortable age to start at. David was a hands-on father who was always good at playing games. Hide and seek became a favorite as soon as Anne could walk, as did "playing in the dark." He wore out the knees on many a pair of trousers playing horses on all fours. Anne always enjoyed traveling from the start and took to our long trips north/south very happily. She is a generous person and did not resent the many bookshop visits with David and would make up her own games to play while he was browsing. She became a keen visitor of castles and National Trust properties, a practice which she continues to this day.

David aged 37, Anne aged 2, on holiday, South London

A new pattern emerged in 1990 which changed life for all of us. David developed what was later found to be ME or Chronic Fatigue Syndrome. Abject tiredness, muscle weakness, and headaches became part of daily life. The condition developed while he was on sabbatical leave and so did not initially interfere with teaching. Gradually all but essential commitments had to be dropped until, in the end, only his job was left with maybe one service on a Sunday, a real deprivation for him. Although he experienced bouts of irrational fear, fortunately he did not suffer too much from the mental confusion that ME victims often undergo. He had to sleep in the living room as his legs could not carry him upstairs and he had to lecture sitting down. The physician did not have much that could help and suggested that if some useful complementary therapy could be found, we should go for it. I had already done some food allergy testing and through various avenues was introduced to Dr. Anna Edstrom in London who specialized in kinesiology. By this technique muscle testing checked out which vitamins and minerals might help. We firmly believe that it was only her therapy that kept David at work through this time. The longest lasting legacy of the ME has been a skewing of David's body clock. He finds it hard to talk sense after 8:30 p.m. and needs to go to bed but tends to wake very early in the morning. This has created stress for him over the years and maybe links with high blood pressure which also requires medication.

Life for us still consisted of being up in Scotland in semester and then having a week at Easter, two weeks at Christmas, and two weeks in the summer down south with our parents who were aging. David and Margaret Lacey spent five years in Edinburgh, but in 1993 moved back to the south coast of England. They went to live in Chichester, West Sussex, near my brother and family. Just as they moved David Lacey had the first of many "turns" which heralded the onset of multi-infarct dementia. Margaret looked after him at home for a while, but eventually he needed more care and went into Funtington Hall nearby where he died in July 1997. Two weeks later, Vera, David's mother, had a heart attack in Nottingham and was taken to hospital. She discharged herself when she knew we were just back from Australia and had a lovely time with us, with all our news, and died of another heart attack in her own home the following day. She had stayed there with wonderful home help from Nottingham City Council carers to the end, just as she had wished. We did not attempt to clear the Covedale Road house at once. The building was an archaeological site with layers of relics in the loft from the past fifty years, starting with the army uniform and gas masks from the Second World War. Eventually we cleared the living area and rented the house out for two years, but trying to keep the house in good condition at a distance of three hundred miles proved impossible and we sold it. And so we lost our midland base which had been so useful on our way south. Now only Margaret was left in Chichester. She managed in her own home with carers for some years but eventually required more support and moved into the nearby Sailaway Rest Home in Bosham, where she died in 2008. Sadly, Sheila, our sister-in-law, died in the following month after many years of fighting cancer. We are very fortunate to know that we helped our three parents live independent lives for as long as possible and we miss the frequent trips south to see them.

Anne grew up surrounded by books and it was a puzzle as to why she did not read them. We were even told at one point that the reason was because we had too many books. She would arrange them beautifully—anything but read. Eventually we realized that there was a reason for this and had her assessed for specific learning disability / dyslexia. She was indeed dyslexic and had the visual gifting that goes with this condition, but the school did not want to acknowledge how this affected her academic learning. We managed to obtain support for her public exams at the age of sixteen, but the school then told her that she could have no help for her next exams and so she left and started beauty therapy at Perth College, continuing all the way to a Higher National Diploma level. She is at present a cosmetologist/beautician and may yet follow a different course now that she understands the impact of dyslexia on how she sees things. Gradually through college and school in Perth she collected an impressive collection of Highers and Advanced Highers, including Advanced Higher classical studies in the top A band, giving the lie to the school's view that she was "only a mediocre student" who, by implication, was not worth helping. David always enjoyed taking Anne to Chinese restaurants during these difficult years and realized that her many gifts were not being appreciated at school. It is so sad to think of all the creative talent that is still being wasted in pupils who see the world slightly differently. It does not seem any better now in many, many schools. Through Anne we have learned just how visually and spatially gifted people with dyslexia can be; and again through Anne we have discovered so much about attachment and the early bonds that form between parent and child, for which we have been grateful.

David aged 56, Anne aged 21, in Waco, Texas

Life took on a new dimension when Anne had a daughter, Rebecca (Becky), in 2004. There were more chances for David to play hide and seek and generally do what grandpas do. David and Becky's specialties at present are shopping trips in Bridge of Allan and Edinburgh and marble playing, both of which have deep roots in David's childhood and both of which lower David's blood pressure considerably! Anne and Becky lived with us for the first few years until they bought their own house in Dunblane. In July 2011 we celebrated forty years of marriage with our ruby wedding anniversary, and in December, Anne married another David, surnamed Cumming, and they had a son, Daniel, in June 2013. David is an excellent addition to the family. Apart from being a very pleasant young man, he has all sorts of practical skills, not just in his own field of electrical engineering design but in many other areas as well. This helps the older David a great deal! And so the family has changed substantially over the years, losing older members and gaining new ones. My brother, Mike, remarried in 2011 and happily now lives with Caroline in her native Switzerland. We have gained a whole new

Swiss and European dimension to the family with wonderful people and locations to visit. Our niece Katharine with husband, James, and her family, and nephew, Jonathan, live down south and always make us welcome.

UNIVERSITY OF STIRLING

The University of Stirling provided the framework for David's career from 1976 onwards. It had opened only in 1967 as the sole Scottish example of a new foundation after the Robbins Report recommended the expansion of British higher education. By 1976, when we arrived, it had around three thousand students; now it has more than ten thousand. Everyone on the staff knew each other to a greater or lesser degree, although university policy was that there should be no separate facilities for staff apart from students. This reflected the thinking of the sixties. At one stage David, as newcomer, was worried that he might even be expected to play in the staff/student football tournaments, but fortunately this did not arise. This "no difference" policy had many advantages, but it made it harder for academics to share ideas with colleagues in other disciplines. There were many ladies' groups active in the mid-seventies, again being open to any women who had connections with the university. I joined the book group, which still flourishes today.

The university is set in a most beautiful campus with Dumyat, a thirteen hundred-foot-high mountain with strong Pictish connections, rising behind it, and the national Wallace Monument from the nineteenth century built on a hill just to the east. All this is within sight of Stirling Castle, perched on a prominent rock and dating from medieval times. The university occupies the site of the Airthrey Estate complete with its own castle and loch (lake) which belonged to the Haldane family who were prominent Baptists in Scotland in the first half of the nineteenth century. This association has given David great satisfaction over the years as well as providing a stunningly beautiful backdrop for his work each day. The campus is generally regarded as one of the finest in the country and attracts many students who want to pursue mountain climbing and outdoor pursuits of all kinds. It also houses the Scottish Institute of Sport and the National Swimming Academy. Stirling was the first UK university to have two semesters a year rather than three terms. Until 2014, the spring semester ran from the second week of February until the middle of June, and the autumn one from early September until Christmas. This was quite hard to adjust to, especially in the twelve-week "low point." But it had advantages in that David could do nonstop research from Christmas for five or six weeks. Having semesters followed the US model and was thought to be quite revolutionary in itself. Eventually all the other British universities flocked to find out how it would run in the United Kingdom and now almost every university has adopted this system, wholly or in part.

University of Stirling

The history department had been set up to provide the teaching of modern history since 1776, starting with the American, French and Industrial Revolutions. It did not offer medieval or early modern courses but it had worldwide coverage. It also included economic history, with Professor Roy Campbell as its redoubtable champion. There had been twenty members of the department, but in 1976 these were reduced to sixteen, with David replacing five people who had left. His remit was to teach modern British history since the late eighteenth century. Scotland had four-year honors degrees. In his second year he was able to introduce Religion, Politics and Society in Nineteenth-Century Britain and the History of Political Thought, based on the courses he had most enjoyed teaching in Cambridge. New lecturers were not allowed to teach final-year special subject courses at first. In fact David did not teach one for the next twelve years. Nowadays newcomers are expected to do this immediately. David did co-teach a final-year course with his friends Anand Chitnis and Neil Tranter on the First Industrial Society from which he learned a great deal. In 2003, a historiography course was introduced which studied various approaches to the writing of history and David coordinated it down to 2013. In most years since the end of the eighties he has run a special subject on William Ewart Gladstone, the British prime minister who remains of enduring interest. David was promoted to be a senior lecturer in 1989, a reader in 1991 and a professor in 1999.

There have been massive changes at the university over the years. In 1976, only 7 percent of the UK population of eighteen-year-olds went to college or university. Now around 50 percent do. The university has had to change from educating a relatively small group of well-qualified students to catering for a mass constituency. Over the years the vast majority of students have been very pleasant. David has come to play an important part in some of their lives. Ken and Linda Jeffrey, for example, first met in David's Religion, Politics and Society course, took his special subject together, and went on to pursue further degrees with him. He spoke at their wedding and we are still in close touch with them and their four children. He also met visiting American students, which first sowed the seed of interest in that country. During the 1980s, however, David was largely confined to the University of Stirling. At that time morale there reached a low when the UK government was discussing cutting or even closing universities. A freeze on jobs meant that David remained the "new boy" in the department until 1990. This seriously skewed the age of the population of university lecturers. In the 1970s and '80s there were many more departmental jobs to be done. In the 1990s, for example, David was chief examiner for many years as well as being deputy head of department. There were also schools liaison officers, admissions, study abroad, careers and health and safety posts to fill from within the department. As the university grew, whole new central departments grew up such as school liaison, human resources, and careers and there was less departmental work.

David aged 29, author of *Patterns in History*

The actual running of the university has changed completely. Committees abounded in the mid-seventies. Each member of staff was on several and it was an excellent way of getting to know people in other departments. Now the institution is run by central administration and the staff have line managers above them to pass decisions down to them. One of the major jobs in each department has been head of department, but once David had started with the ME it was clear that he would never be fit enough to withstand the pressures of this job.

Another huge change has been the arrival of computers. In 1976 computers hardly affected anyone's lives in the department. Secretaries with typewriters at first and then word processors carried out most administrative tasks and lecturers needed to find a typist to type their books. (This had one advantage. Writing had to be finished by an agreed date and sometimes typos corrected and alterations paid for. And so there was a huge incentive to get it right first time. Nowadays there is endless scope for moving everything round *ad infinitum* and people are finding it harder and harder to finish.) Now each lecturer has his own PC and is expected to type all his own material and carry out administrative tasks online. Some aspects of this trouble David a great deal. Filling in complicated online forms for funding or for references can irritate him a lot, especially when categories do not fit history. All sorts of information have to be put on student websites. He has not remained a dinosaur with computers, refusing to use them, but the tasks he is required to do are often beyond what he is trained for. The constant stream of e-mails with requests from all round the world can be overwhelming even without the spam ones. Too much use of the computer can give him severe headaches.

Teacher training did not figure largely in higher education in the mid-seventies. You were expected to learn chiefly on the job. David was sent on a minimal three-day course to learn his trade. He remembers the futility of much of the training, symbolized by repeated references by an education lecturer to what "Postlethwaite found at Purdue," though the identity of Postlethwaite and what he discovered were never explained, nor had David heard of Purdue University at that stage. Eventually, in 1997, David acted as a member of the Teaching Quality Assessment team sent to investigate the history departments at the universities of Edinburgh, Glasgow, and St. Andrews on the first occasion that disciplines were subject to external scrutiny. He enjoyed exercising his powers to call for persons and papers, discovering that standards were in general excellent. Now David values various teaching methods, but mainly loves to split a group in two and arrange for each side to argue its case with evidence and then reach conclusions. That reflects what he believes that writing a history essay should be. Once students have practiced taking sides in a debate, the idea is that it should be easier for them to write their essays and dissertations.

David's essay technique is the one that he uses on a larger scale for his academic papers and published books. There is a definite pattern here. First he writes a plan, putting everything he wants to include on one side of a sheet of paper. Often the topic will be one where there are two or more sides to a debate. David decides which way the evidence points overall and which side he is going to favor in the end. Then he writes up the factors pointing against his conclusion, a paragraph for each, starting with the least weighty and ending with the most. Then he lists the factors supporting the conclusion, again going from the least to the most persuasive, before summarizing the overall argument. He expects conclusions in essays written by students to be firm, taking, with due qualifications, a particular point of view! It is this ability to master the subject, weighing up both sides and arguing for one point of view on the basis of clear evidence, which is the most transferable skill in the job market. Many business leaders train in history and become able assessors of relevant factors in their work. The value of this experience could be deployed much more in the "What is the use of history?" debate. (For a talk by David on "The Use of History," see appendix 1.)

THE WIDER SCOTTISH SCENE

The move to Stirling opened up other opportunities in history. He was able to take initiatives within Scotland. Very quickly David started a Scottish group of the Historians' Study Group, now called the Christianity and History Forum, which he had enjoyed attending in London. This group for committed Christian historians started to meet twice a year, often in Stirling. In those days numbers were large as American research students would come through from Edinburgh. David was secretary of the group for twenty-five years. It still meets once a year. Although there are now smaller numbers, those attending value the chance to think through the relation of their Christian faith to the history in which they work. Sometimes David is still able to attend the group that meets in London or elsewhere in England and Wales and remains on the committee. In alternate years there has been a study conference, long held at Offa House in the West Midlands (now sadly closed), where many Christian historians have come together. New venues are now in use. David often says he feels more in tune there than anywhere else. Over the years preparing talks to give to this group has made David hone his thinking.

At the same time he started the Scottish Baptist History Project (SBHP), not as a branch of the Baptist Historical Society (BHS), but as an organization supplementary to it. He remains on the committee of the BHS, which normally meets in London, and tries to attend as many meetings as distance allows. At the BHS he continued to meet Dr. Ernest Payne, its president down to his death in 1980, who then left David his complete set of the *Baptist Quarterly*. The SBHP holds two meetings a year where three speakers read papers on various aspects of Baptist history, particularly in Scotland. In 2009, David handed over the secretaryship to the Reverend Brian Talbot, minister of Broughty Ferry Baptist Church, who had completed a PhD with David and is the archivist of the Baptist Union of Scotland. One of the tasks of the project is to support churches holding special celebrations. For example, in 2000, a group went up to the very north of

Scotland to help Keiss Baptist Church, the oldest continuing church in the denomination, to hold its two hundred and fiftieth anniversary.

Keiss Baptist Church, Sutherland, on its 250th anniversary

More recently in 2007, David and David Brown, then of Strathclyde University, started a series of Conferences on Modern British History. These are held in June in different Scottish universities and are designed to foster interaction between academics teaching in university posts and postgraduate students working in the period since the late eighteenth century. The conferences cover all types of history, political, social, and economic, but David was glad when, owing to popular demand, there were two spin-off conferences on religion. The integration of Christian history into mainstream history has remained a long-term preoccupation.

At Stirling David continued to take an interest in politics. Each day he read the *Times* and, after it started to be published, the *Independent*, usually last thing at night after his Bible reading. This kept him up-to-date with current affairs. At the 1987 general election the Stirling Council of Churches asked him to talk on the options available to voters. One party sent agents along to take notes in case they found undue partisanship, but there were no protests, which gave David considerable satisfaction. At the general election in 1997 he preached a sermon at Stirling Baptist Church on the Sunday before voting was to take place, laying stress, as a member of the religious studies department remarked, on the "intermediate principles" between theological convictions and political policies. He never joined a political party, but in 2014 was asked to give an introductory talk on nationhood before rival MSPs (Members of the Scottish Parliament) put forward their opposing views on which way people should vote at the forthcoming referendum on Scottish independence. He felt strongly on this issue but managed to restrain himself—just! He becomes troubled when constant criticism in the media is hurled at Members of the UK Parliament whom he believes, by and large, to be conscientious and underpaid for what they do. He is a very rare specimen of someone who actually becomes excited when party political broadcasts are about to come on television!

THE UK SCENE

David's activities were not confined to Scotland. Apart from the Baptist Historical Society and the Historians' Study Group, David has had a long association with the Ecclesiastical History Society (EHS). Formed in 1961 by historians from all over the United Kingdom, the society is intended to encourage the study of church history in all periods. It has proved a useful way for him to keep in touch with his medieval and early modern interests to balance the largely modern approach of Stirling. When David first attended its summer conference in 1970, the society contained some of the great names in the field, such as Professor Owen Chadwick, who held chairs at Cambridge. (Amazingly Professor Chadwick was still at a meeting of the board of the *Journal of Ecclesiastical History* that David attended in 2012.) Professor Reg Ward was president that year. As a man proud of his Primitive Methodist lineage, he gave David an illustration of what a Nonconformist can achieve, very much as Geoffrey Cushing had done all those years previously in Nottingham High School, and remained a role model for him until his death a few years ago. When David was president of the EHS in 2006/07, he proposed that the fiftieth anniversary of the society should be celebrated in a history which Stella Fletcher, the society's secretary, then wrote. It appeared to much enthusiasm in 2011. David gave a lecture at the fiftieth-anniversary conference that year, staying in Tom Quad, Christ Church, Oxford, the very quad where Gladstone had lived as an undergraduate. He was also awarded a prestigious fellowship of the society, which is a rare honor. He is very proud of his complete set of the society's annual volumes, *Studies in Church History*, one of the very few in private hands.

Another fascinating activity within the United Kingdom has been research on Nonconformist Members of Parliament. The project began when the Baptist Historical Society commissioned David in the late 1970s to catalog all the members of the denomination who have served in Parliament. That led to three articles in the *Baptist Quarterly* in the 1980s. He was later invited to give the annual lectures to the United Reformed Church History Society and the Unitarian Historical Society and so he tried to identify and discuss all the nineteenth-century MPs from Congregationalism (which appeared in a short book) and Unitarianism. This project made him interested in such men as David Lloyd George, the wartime prime minister with roots in the Churches of Christ, and so he was fascinated later to visit Lloyd George's nephew, William George, still a practicing solicitor in the 1990s, who remembered being taken to 10 Downing Street as a child.

One of the sources for biographical details on Nonconformist MPs was Dr. Williams's Library in Bloomsbury, central London, an atmospheric mid-nineteenth-century building with dark wooden shelving and a variety of stairways that is sometimes used for film sets. From 2004 the library formed an alliance with Queen Mary, University of London, to create Dr. William's Centre for Dissenting Studies. David spoke at its conferences and workshops, sat on its academic advisory board and shared in the massive project for a history of Dissenting academies from 1660 to 1860. Although the volume on that subject is yet to appear, the centre has been responsible for a tornado of academic activity that, to David's satisfaction, has placed Nonconformity much more centrally on the scholarly map.

CHRISTIAN FAITH

A phrase from the Bible which had meant a great deal to David since college days was *Dominus providebit*, "the Lord will provide," from Genesis 22:14. It was carved into the stone of Chapel Court in Jesus College and on the day when David was going to Scotland for his interview at Stirling in 1976, he saw it inscribed on a building close to the National Library in Edinburgh. The principle has been important to him throughout. He has preached on it several times. Provision was certainly made for him in Scotland. From the start in Stirling David owed a great deal to the Reverend James Taylor, who was minister of Stirling Baptist Church where we became members in 1976. Deeply influenced by the leading evangelical Anglican, John Stott, James Taylor was a careful expository preacher as well as being a kind and witty man. David was eventually to deliver James Taylor's eulogy at his funeral in 2012 and wrote his obituary for the *Herald* newspaper.

During the earlier years in Stirling the rhythm of family life was molded to a great extent by Stirling Baptist Church. David entered fully into local church life. He became a deacon at the church in the late seventies, serving with friends such as Hugh McWhinnie, and leader of a house group, regularly visiting members in their homes. He also joined in the affairs of the Central Baptist Association that linked the Baptist churches of the area, becoming its president in 1980. But from the start of the 1990s his participation became strictly limited by his ME. Since then his activities have usually had to stop by 8:30 and so he had to resign as a deacon and could only attend church meeting until midway through its evening sessions. Before he had to cut down his activities, however, David often spoke at Christian Unions (CUs) in Scotland during the 1980s. He had been a member of the Cambridge CU and so it was natural to support the Stirling equivalent, but he also regularly traveled to the flourishing evangelical student bodies elsewhere. Aberdeen was particularly welcoming. As a result he served as a vice president of the Universities and Colleges Christian Fellowship, the umbrella organization for CUs, between 1987 and 1992. One very helpful experience was attending the staff Bible study on the university campus. Numbers were small, but friendships developed as people of different theological persuasions from various disciplines contributed their perspectives on scripture.

One great difference in Scotland when we came was that smaller local Baptist churches tended to have ministers, a very different situation from in Cambridgeshire. That has meant there have been far fewer opportunities to preach. Sometimes during vacancies David has helped local Baptist churches, for example at Peebles and Cumbernauld, and he always finds preparing sermons very helpful for his own faith. We still have notes for all his sermons, written of course in his own shorthand.

David continued his regimen of daily personal prayer and self-examination and intercession. For many years he used a commentary every evening. He liked reading works such as Gerhard von Rad's commentary on Genesis and Karl Barth's on Romans devotionally, but now he normally dispenses with any commentary. He will choose a book of the Bible to study. Some days he will study a whole chapter, sometimes just one verse. He loves to wrestle with difficult passages in the Bible such as Leviticus. He has a very deep knowledge of theology and finds it hard to believe at times that not everyone has studied the books of the Bible as often as he has.

Since 1997, the Reverend Dr. Alasdair Black has been minister of Stirling Baptist Church and David has greatly enjoyed his preaching, which reflects his unusually wide range of interests. In the summer of 2013, for example, he took David on an afternoon car trip to view places relating to early Scottish Christianity and his preferred candidate for the site of the battle of Mons Graupius of AD 79 as reported by the Roman historian Tacitus. Other interests are the birth narratives of the gospels and all aspects of the history of the church in Scotland. He combines a profound learning with an unusual degree of accessibility. He and his wife, Susan, have become good friends.

TRAVELS AND CONFERENCES

We had no idea when David began in Stirling that travel would open up not only within the United Kingdom but also across the world. The first invitation came from Belfast in Northern Ireland in 1980 to speak at the Union Theological College. The city was a troubled place at that time and so the trip seemed a little risky from the start. Then the flight was canceled because of fog and so the only way to reach the lecture next morning was to catch the ancient, drafty train from Glasgow to Stranraer on the southwest coast of Scotland and then the ferry to Larne in Northern Ireland. David's cabin was next to the loading machinery putting cargo on board and so it was a very bleary-eyed lecturer that appeared next morning in Belfast! This trip brought home to him some of the realities of the political and sectarian violence that had been troubling the land. Regular visits to the city for examining, hosted by Finlay Holmes of the Union Theological College, proved to be very worthwhile over the next few years.

It seemed unlikely that any more travel would come David's way. In 1985, however, the Ecclesiastical History Society nominated him to go to Stuttgart to speak at the International Historical Congress. As I waved him off from the bus station in Bournemouth where Anne and I were staying with my parents, it seemed a highly exotic adventure, but then in 1989 David visited America for the first time. After one night at Harvard, he spoke at Gordon College, Massachusetts, and was overjoyed when he was offered eighty volumes that were no longer needed. Then he went on to Wheaton College, Illinois, to speak; from there he traveled to Regent College,

Vancouver, to give a series of Staley lectures. In 1990 he taught for a week at the University of Birmingham, Alabama, having met Ed Harrell, the head of history there, at the Wheaton conference. This was his first visit to the South, but soon afterwards he also went to Duke University, North Carolina, to attend a conference run by George Marsden on university history. The year of 1992 saw David at Vancouver again and he returned several times to conferences at Wheaton College near Chicago. In 1994 David taught at a summer school for young scholars at Notre Dame University, South Bend, Indiana, and Anne and I joined him for ten days before flying to Disney World in Florida. As I had had a hysterectomy a few weeks beforehand, the traveling was quite an ordeal and Anne well remembers crossing Chicago O'Hare Airport at top speed with me being pushed in a wheelchair and her nine-year-old legs running as fast as they could to keep up! She also loved playing in the sprinklers on the Notre Dame campus and swimming in people's pools. This was when she first resolved to live in the United States! In 1995 David and Anne flew back to Chicago, David to a conference and Anne to stay with a friend she had made. During these years David developed his fascination with the similarities and differences between the United Kingdom and the United States. He often says that he would like to restore the kingdom of Atlantis, place it exactly halfway between the two countries and fill it with the best of both.

These American trips seemed exciting enough, but more distant lands were beckoning. Hoffie Hofmeyr and David had met at Wheaton, and in 1995 Hoffie invited him to come to South Africa to teach part of a course on evangelicalism at the University of Pretoria. Hardly anyone had been visiting South Africa in the apartheid years and now the Queen and David were both invited with the same purpose—to show that the country was returning to mainstream international life. The day before David set off, South Africa won the rugby World Cup, and Hoffie phoned straight afterwards to say how much they were looking forward to the visit. David even managed to visit a wildlife park where extra vaccinations were not required. He had been advised to avoid unnecessary ones because of his ME, which rules out many destinations for him.

After South Africa various other countries came up. In 1995, for example, David flew to Kingston, Ontario, to attend a conference on Canadian evangelicalism organized by George Rawlyk. George was an outstanding Baptist historian for whom David always had a great respect. It was a great shock when, in November 1996, he died as a result of a car accident as he was returning home from the airport after a visit to us. Just before he left Scotland he had taken us out to a wonderful meal in Bridge of Allan and had spent some hours with David discussing plans for the first International Conference on Baptist Studies.

The summer of 1997 saw the whole family on the move again. We flew via Los Angeles to New Zealand, where we first visited an ex-teacher of mine from school. The jet lag was dire. It is the only time I have seen David fall asleep when walking! But the country was beautiful. Then to Brisbane, Australia, to stay with Paul and Audrey Harrison, our ex-minister from Cambridge and his wife. David then flew to Melbourne, where he found the best used bookstores anywhere, while Anne, always an enthusiastic traveler, and I went sightseeing around Cairns and the Great Barrier Reef. I met up with David in Sydney and on the first day we lost each other in one of the main shopping streets. As I had only flown in that day David was not sure that I knew the name of the hotel. Fortunately I remembered it and we both phoned the hotel who directed us to meet, but not before David had reported the loss of his wife to the local police office, where they roared with laughter and congratulated him very warmly! This did not encourage David very much. I was never keen on Sydney after that. David attended a conference on global evangelicalism where he celebrated his forty-eighth birthday and we stayed in a flat with a very soggy water bed and an amphibian called an axolotl which we had to look after. Then we traveled to Flinders University in Adelaide where Anne and I felt colder than we had ever done. My father died back home in the United Kingdom while we were in Adelaide, but the funeral was postponed for ten days so that we could return in time to attend. We had a stopover in Fiji on the way back in stormy weather which made the coconuts bounce off the trees. Somehow some local Christian historians discovered that David was there and asked him to go to the University of the South Pacific in the capital, Suva, to give a paper. They sent a government car to convey him there and that caused quite a stir at the holiday village. We experienced how fanatical the Fijians were about rugby. The main question we were asked in the remotest spots was whether we had been to Cardiff Arms Park (the Welsh Rugby ground) to see the amazing new sliding roof which could cover the stadium in wet weather.

In 1998 we all stayed at Wheaton Square near Wheaton College, Illinois, while David worked on material on American evangelicalism and Anne and I experienced the wonders of Chicago and the local shopping facilities. In 1999 David traveled to Nova Scotia for the first time, to Acadia

University, for a pair of endowed lectures. The more specialized a person's research area becomes, the fewer people are working on it. David's travels showed him that scholars of evangelicalism scattered around the world are often convinced that somewhere else there must be a center where many of them meet and have deep discussions on their subject. However, David has never found this mythical center and no longer believes it exists. Travel does give opportunities to meet kindred spirits and e-mail enables them to keep in touch far more easily than in the past.

Conferences both national and international have played a large part in the Stirling years. There was a whole series of conferences in the 1990s held by the Institute for the Study of American Evangelicals under Mark Noll's leadership at Wheaton College. David has been part of this network since then. Many of the same people have been involved in the North Atlantic Missiology project funded by the Pew Trust. This turned into the Currents in World Christianity project administered by a good friend, Brian Stanley, later Professor of World Christianity at New College, Edinburgh. Brian and his wife, Rosey, now live within easy visiting distance, a pleasure for all of us. David attended the Currents in World Christianity conferences in Oxford, South Africa, and Cambridge. This project was really important in transforming missionary history into a proper historical discipline. In the years 2008–2009 David ran the Evangelicalism and Fundamentalism in Britain Project, funded by the Religion and Society Project of the Arts and Humanities Research Council and the Economic and Social Research Council. Five conferences were held and a book of findings was published in 2013 called *Evangelicalism and Fundamentalism in the United Kingdom during the Twentieth Century*.

David lecturing at the Calvin Quatercentenary Conference, Geneva, 2009

One of the most exciting strings of conferences has been the series of International Conferences on Baptist Studies. He started the first one in 1997, but the venture had been planned with George Rawlyk before his untimely death. David has always seen ICOBS as a tribute to George. The plan was not that it should be a small group of Baptist antiquarians, but that good history should be produced on the Baptist past and made available to all. ICOBS meets every three years, alternating between North America and the rest of the world. Each time the proceedings have been published, with David editing the first volume, *The Gospel in the World: International Baptist Studies* (2002), and coediting a later one, *Interfaces: Baptists and Others: International Baptist Studies* (2013). Usually there are about a hundred attenders with the largest contingent often from Scotland. These conferences have brought Baptists together from many different countries.

RESEARCH STUDENTS

One of the most rewarding experiences over the time in Stirling has been that of supervising postgraduate students for their PhDs. This new pattern emerged in the late 1980s. The first postgraduate was a homegrown Stirling student, Julie Rugg, who set an amazingly high standard. Apart from her now renowned work in York on cemeteries and housing policy, she has gone on to publish two excellent books on books and book collecting and so she holds a special place in David's estimation. It is possible to do post-doctoral work straight after a first degree in the United Kingdom and also to study part-time at Stirling and so increasing numbers of American postgraduates have worked with David. Often they have spent one or two years here full-time before continuing part-time in the United States. It would be invidious to single people out. Suffice it to say that these students have almost always been a pleasure to work with and many have become friends. David is a hard taskmaster as supervisor. He follows the guidance given by my father for David's own PhD and requires regular written work along the way. Sometimes students who have not done this have serious threshold problems when it comes to writing the thesis up. Some of the PhD students have gone on to academic posts, like Tim Larsen, Linda Wilson, John Maiden, and Jonathan Yeager, and some have continued or taken up Christian ministry such as John D'Elia, Brian Talbot, and Ken Jeffrey. Ian Randall and Robert Strivens have gone into theological teaching; Charlie Phillips and Larry Eskridge have occupied very responsible administrative posts within Christian institutions in the United States. Many others have just found their daily life enriched by studying a subject in greater depth. Altogether David has supervised thirty students who have taken their PhDs and there are six still in the process.

Usually he has a fair idea of the topic on which PhD research is undertaken. He also has supervised many final-year undergraduate dissertations and master's degrees, but they may be from a far wider field. Topics have varied from the twentieth-century use of the word "crusade" to Chinese film! As ever, David wades into a new area with enthusiasm. He has also acted as external examiner for over seventy PhDs in other universities and believes in giving the candidate a thorough grilling since this, he insists, is the peak of the UK education system. He has valued the way in which the external examining system has brought him together with colleagues in similar fields, such as Clyde Binfield of Sheffield and Densil Morgan, now of Lampeter.

BAYLOR UNIVERSITY, TEXAS

Within the Stirling section of this book, Baylor University needs to find a place. Situated in Waco, Texas, the university was founded in 1845 by Judge Baylor as a college to serve the Baptists of Texas. Around 2000 the university authorities formed a "2012" vision by which they aimed to turn the institution into a front-rank research university while retaining its Christian profession. In 2002 they asked David to go out for a week to see if we would move there full-time. We seriously considered that possibility during a whole semester in the fall of 2003, but a permanent settlement in Texas was not practical for family reasons. Nevertheless a new rhythm of life emerged. David was invited out for the fall semesters of 2003, 2005, 2007, 2009, and 2011 to provide teaching for postgraduates in the history department and for Truett Seminary, the Baptist ministerial training institution on the campus. I visited for six weeks or so in the middle and Anne and family came for shorter or longer periods. David has taught Gladstone Studies and a Baptist Identity course together with, on one occasion, British Evangelicalism.

Family group in Waco, Texas, 2009: Eileen, Becky, David, David Cumming, Anne

The weather in Waco is amazingly hot, especially when compared with Scotland. It is normally well over 100 Fahrenheit for the first month David is in Texas, which is not ideal. We have met some wonderful people on our visits and the opportunities for visiting other church services are second to none. Waco itself has eighty-three Baptist churches, as well as dozens of Methodist buildings, Churches of Christ, and so on. Every Sunday morning we would attend First Baptist, Waco, and in the evening we would visit a whole range of other churches such as the Landmark Baptists. We especially enjoy the small African American churches in East Waco; in some areas there is one on nearly every street corner. All these services have provided many pages of note taking for David's research! Texas has been a constant source of surprise to us. We knew of Dallas and Houston and we knew Texas was big, but we did not realize that there are hundreds of miles of country roads with small decaying Victorian townships dotted at intervals which, with their strong flavor of time past, are particularly exciting for David. In the United Kingdom, older buildings are usually demolished to make way for new structures, but there is so much space in Texas that they just erect something new next door and so you can see continuity of buildings. Waco itself has a host of eating places. David became very fond of Texas barbeque beef as well as his usual Chinese preferences. The city suffered greatly through being unfairly linked by the media to the protracted and tragic siege by the federal agents of the Branch Davidian community, fourteen miles away in a place unknown to the vast majority of Waco residents.

From Waco, David has visited other universities, such as Oklahoma Baptist University, Southern Methodist University in Dallas, the University of Tennessee, Chattanooga, and many others. The travel has been eventful at times. Once when he was due to fly to a conference, fortunately not to speak, in Portland, Oregon, he found on arrival at Dallas Fort Worth Airport that he had been booked to Portland, Maine, the whole width of the United States away! He cancelled the Oregon booking and went on to enjoy a vacation in New England in the fall instead.

BOOK WRITING

So what has been the pattern of his book writing? After David's first literary effort, written when he was nine, there was a gap, although he did write a diary from the ages of fifteen to nineteen. He also did research on the two subjects of public health and the effects of war for the Nottingham local history prize in the first and second year of the sixth form at the High School (which he won). When A levels were safely over, David wanted a larger historical project of his own to work on. He had two ideas: some research on the seventeenth- and eighteenth-century heraldic hatchments in the parish churches of Nottinghamshire, following on from his interest in heraldry, or a history of his own church, Queensberry Street Baptist Church, Old Basford, Nottingham. Unsure which to choose, he asked for advice from the secretary of the Thoroton Society, who encouraged him to do the second. I remain profoundly glad that he did not pursue the hatchments as I have never enthused about heraldry. And so David set out on a substantial local history project, interviewing older members of the church, people who had left thirty years before, and members whose grandparents started the church and who remembered stories from the early days. He developed various techniques that he still uses, such as showing a photo of a person involved in the earlier years and seeing what memories it prompts. He also learned some of the pitfalls of recent history, such as the way people want their own bit of the story to be given far more coverage than any other! He tried to understand the whole picture and did a great deal of research. The project then went on hold for the next eight years until his first semester in Stirling in 1976, by which time it was urgent to finish since the church centenary was fast approaching. It was published in time in 1977.

InterVarsity Press had meanwhile approached David to write a handbook for Christian students of history and he fairly quickly wrote *Patterns in History* during the next couple of years. The aim was to give an account from a Christian standpoint of the changing perspectives on what history is, and so it deals with large movements such as the legacy of the Enlightenment and Romanticism. *Patterns*, published in 1979, is still in print and is likely to be updated soon. It is used in historiography courses in various countries in secular universities as well as Christian institutions. It was translated in South Korea and was apparently in the list of Top Ten Books one Christmas. *Patterns* still provides a perspective into which phenomena from every period of history can be fitted. Postmodernism is likely to be added in the update and will give an understanding of a movement that can be very hard to grasp. *Patterns* has been the broad canvas against which exchanges of ideas and local events have been studied in what David now calls his macro/micro approach to history.

While David was doing his PhD on the "Nonconformist Conscience," he researched the way that Methodists, Congregationalists, Baptists, and Quakers (collectively the Nonconformists) took part in the political process between 1886 and 1902. At the end he remained ambivalent about what was done by the people involved, respecting their aims but feeling uneasy about some of their methods. He preferred those used by William Wilberforce, such as timely persuasion and discreet pressure. (For a sermon on William Wilberforce, see appendix 2.) The resulting book, *The Nonconformist Conscience*, covering a much longer timescale, from 1870 to 1914, was published in 1982.

From this book two main consequences flowed. First, David came to appreciate that he should study more about William Gladstone, the prime

The Stirling Years

minister of the United Kingdom who held office four times and had been a great hero of the Nonconformists. David, as usual, wanted to find out why. Second, he decided that he needed to study evangelicalism, the predominant theological outlook of the chapels at that time that shaped their life and had a huge influence on society.

After a lengthy discussion one sunny afternoon in the beautiful garden of Clevedon Court, a National Trust property near Bristol, we decided that David should write a history of evangelicalism in Britain quickly before getting on with a study of Gladstone. He managed to finish *Evangelicalism in Modern Britain* for it to be published by Unwin Hyman in 1989. Originally he thought it would start at 1800, but then realized he needed to examine the movement from the 1730s onwards. Chapter 1 of the book contains the now famous fourfold definition of the subject, known as the "Bebbington quadrilateral," which is widely used when people want a definition of evangelicalism. After a friend from Cambridge had asked him to speak on the Nonconformist Conscience at his church in around 1979, David realized that to do that he had to define evangelicalism. He came up with "orthodox and evangelistic Protestantism" but realized that would not do. And so, using the evidence of past and present, he came up with the four defining features that evangelicals emphasize:

1. The Bible
2. The Cross
3. Conversion
4. Activism.

It is for this batch of four points that he has become best known. They were never intended to be the last word on the subject, but they seem to have struck a chord.

Evangelicalism in Modern Britain, 1989

During the 1980s David edited a multi-authored book called *The Baptists in Scotland*, a collection of chapters on the various regions of the country with four chronological studies of broad historical developments. Then in 1988 he attended a conference in Oxford under the auspices of the C. S. Lewis Society, a largely American organization, where he spoke on universities in Europe from the eleventh century to the present day. The resulting paper eventually appeared in print in 2011! The conference, however, was important in forging links with the United States. Mark Noll, then of Wheaton College, Illinois, and now of Notre Dame University, Indiana, arranged for David to speak at Wheaton, where he argued that evangelicalism, far from being a staunch foe of the Enlightenment of the eighteenth century, was in fact deeply molded by it. That view, novel at the time, has gradually become the received opinion.

The Stirling Years

Then David researched, wrote, and taught Gladstone. Mark Noll asked for a volume for his Eerdmans Library of Christian Biography series and David chose to write on Gladstone. *William Ewart Gladstone: Faith and Politics in Victorian Britain* (1993) tried to show that as a Christian statesman it is possible to be a conservative in religion as well as a liberal in politics. By this time ME was slowing David down and he spent a long time digging among the Gladstone papers. He often visited Gladstone's Library (then known as St. Deiniol's). Set in Hawarden, just in Flintshire in Wales in the same village as Hawarden Castle where Gladstone lived for many years, the building was put up to house his extensive library. Indeed Gladstone transported his books personally in wheelbarrows up from the castle to the new building because he would not entrust them to anyone else! David has always felt a special affinity with Mr. G in this respect. Accommodation at the library, which is designed to give study opportunities to researchers, has now been brought up to Welsh Tourist Board standards and is a wonderfully quiet place to stay with a whole variety of interesting people in residence. There David prepared much of his book *The Mind of Gladstone*. This work examined the three main preoccupations of Gladstone's intellectual life—theology, Homer, and political thought—and involved the extensive reading of many of Gladstone's manuscripts including his sermons. David concluded that the three strands are interrelated and inseparable. David has twice delivered the Founder's Day lecture at St. Deiniol's. On the first occasion we stayed at the castle with the current Sir William, the great-grandson of the prime minister. We spent our silver wedding anniversary in 1996 at the service of thanksgiving in Hawarden Church, singing Gladstone's translation into Latin of the hymn "Rock of Ages," which was quite an experience. The second time David gave the lecture was in 2004. He was researching in Cambridge three days before the lecture when he was phoned to ask if he could speak because that year's lecturer had canceled. He just happened to have a spare lecture on Gladstone in his briefcase and delivered that on Gladstonian Liberalism.

Gladstone studies continued. On the centenary of Gladstone's death in 1998 David organized a conference at University College, Chester, along with Roger Swift and they secured some excellent speakers including Colin Matthew, who had recently completed the mammoth task of editing the Gladstone diaries. In 2009, the bicentenary of Gladstone's birth was celebrated with another conference in Chester. David coedited the *Gladstone Centenary Essays* that had grown out of the first conference and wrote a foreword to the papers from the second. He was made a fellow of the library, which he regards as a great honor.

In 1992 *Victorian Nonconformity* appeared and has remained popular, especially with the Open University. This was to meet the need for a very brief introduction for students about nineteenth-century Nonconformity which very few understood. The book was reissued in revised form in America as well as Britain in 2011. He also assembled a collection of primary documents on the nineteenth century for *Protestant Nonconformist Texts* (2006) which took five years to appear but which is likely to be reprinted soon.

In 2005 *The Dominance of Evangelicalism* appeared. It had been made possible by David's travels in the 1990s when he collected material for it from various repositories around the world. The book is a history of the global evangelical movement of the second half of the nineteenth century and is part of a series edited by Mark Noll and David. It was going to contain a chapter on revivals, but David became so excited in preparing for that chapter that he realized they warranted a whole book to themselves. This was the origin of the Victorian revivals book of 2012. Appearing as *Victorian Religious Revivals*, this volume examines seven case studies of revivals across the world ranging from 1841 to 1880. Instead of generalizing about revivals as so many books have done, it tries to investigate everything that can be discovered about these events both at macro and micro level. The micro, what local people are saying and thinking at a particular time, is the best way of illustrating the macro. This is where the large movements such as the Enlightenment and Romanticism from *Patterns* can be seen affecting the attitudes of individuals in the fishing villages of Cornwall and Nova Scotia or in the mining settlements of South Australia.

David's course on Baptist Identity at Truett Seminary in Baylor University forced him to come to terms with the main themes of American Baptist history. American and British developments, he became convinced, were mutually illuminating. The outcome was a history of Baptists worldwide which was published by Baylor University Press in 2010 as *Baptists through the Centuries: A History of a Global People*. David taught this subject and wrote about it in tandem, each week producing a chapter on the same subject as his seminar. It was an exhausting but fulfilling technique for book production.

These then are the books. Apart from them there have been hundreds of papers given around the world. Some have turned into books. Some have appeared in journals and some still lie hidden.

BOOKS AND BOOK COLLECTING

Book collecting continued unabated. Space soon became a problem. When I had first known David and visited the house in Nottingham, his bed was an island in the middle of metal shelves full of books. The collection has become more focused, but I did question from the start why a *Dictionary of the Hausa Language* had pride of place. Now he still buys in bulk but concentrates on the areas he is most interested in. At first my parents looked askance at the book collection, fearing that the books would absorb all our money! There is a story of a man sent out to buy the Christmas turkey who returns with an attractive book instead. David could easily do that! He regards his books with great respect. In other homes in Nottingham books could sometimes be smeared with butter or jam, but he is scrupulous to keep his books safe and clean. He still washes his hands before handling his books and prefers anyone else to do the same. He practically needs to inspect the home of anyone borrowing them! Why? Not because of the books themselves, but because he regards them in the same way as John Milton described them, as "the precious life blood of a master spirit," and has the same respect for the authors as he was taught to have for people. It was therefore a catastrophe when, in 2000, a frozen pipe burst above his room at work, flooding the floor and deluging a bay full of books. A large number had to be put in the freezer at home to eliminate the water before they were dried over several days in cold air flows. Astonishingly the same thing happened eleven years later, again between Christmas and New Year, and even more damage was done. The Welsh section was particularly wet. Since the university disclaimed responsibility and insurance would have been prohibitive, there was only nominal compensation the first time and none the second. But many were in any case irreplaceable; and none was damaged beyond all use.

David in secondhand bookshop, Eastbourne, Sussex, 1983

Over the last forty years David has built up an extensive collection. His nineteenth-century biography section holds many books essential to his work. He can use up to a hundred books a day when writing a book or article. He loves biographies of obscure Primitive Methodist preachers which have little meaning to the bookseller and are therefore cheap but who will provide him with raw material to illustrate his points. Other specialisms include denominational and local history and political and historical thought. Our north-south journeys have been wonderful for finding out-of-the-way bookshops across a wide area of the country.

Sadly now the Internet is changing the shape of book buying and small bookshops are closing fast. But there are still ones to be found both in Britain and abroad. David discovered a wonderful quotation, from Anatole France, in one of the books that Julie Rugg compiled. "I scarcely ever pass by [booksellers'] boxes without picking out of one of them some old book which I had always been in need of up to that very moment without any suspicion of the fact on my part." When the booksellers ask, "Are you looking for anything in particular?" David will answer, "1,001 things but I don't know what they are yet." The book collecting serves as his hobby, his thrill of the chase, his raw material for the generation of patterns. He loves to find a book at one shop that is twice the price of one he has already bought at another. He is not so keen on the other way round! He loves the variety of shops and their owners that he meets. Many secondhand bookshop keepers are unusual people. Some are reluctant to sell their wares and many, many of them claim to have thousands and thousands in another place that nobody can view yet. He likes the shop in Southport which still wraps purchases in brown paper. He values enormously the Bookaid shops in Ranskill, Barnard Castle, Warrington, and Sydenham where many of the sorts of book he uses most can be bought at very reasonable prices. And he delights in Yr Hen Bost, a secondhand bookshop in the unexpected setting of Blaenau Ffestiniog in north Wales, which holds a splendid stock of Nonconformist books. The drawback is that many of them are written in Welsh, which he does not read, but David has bought only two or three volumes in that language. There is a storage room across the street; and on one occasion the kindly proprietor welcomed us to lunch so that David could view the supplementary holdings in the basement and attic of his home. As an added extra, the bookseller invited a friend, a Scotch Baptist elder, to meet us—particularly intriguing since the Scotch Baptist denomination survives only in north Wales.

Fortunately the books, though bulky, have not been over-expensive. David likes Nonconformist memoirs, for example, which nobody else wants. Further afield, he loves the Brattle Book Shop in Boston, United States, which offers a splendid range of nineteenth-century texts at reasonable prices. He has attended only two books auctions, when, in 2008, the library of the Gladstone family house, Fasque, in Kincardineshire, was for sale. He managed to buy the Bible belonging to Anne, Gladstone's older sister, containing her notes in the margin, and also a set of the sermons of an Edinburgh minister presented by the nine-year-old Gladstone, "their dutiful and affectionate son," to his parents. Although not expensive in themselves, the books have required the garage at home to be converted, and with retirement on the horizon a new library has been built in our garden. Some men need sheds when they retire. David needs his books close by. They are his friends and a source of inspiration for his research and writing which I anticipate he will want to do as long as he is able.

NOTES ON SERVICES

Maybe David's greatest legacy will not be the "quadrilateral" but his continuous series of notes on church services. Started in the mid-1960s, they have been with him in one way or another ever since. The only service not written down was our wedding when I threatened instant divorce if he did! These are the notebooks in which he records the proceedings at the worship he attends. The sequence of songs, prayers, and sermons is timed; the contents of the sermon are copied down in detail; the physical setting is described; and any idiosyncrasies—or even heresies—are taken down. There are equivalent records of the liturgical pattern in High Church services, whether Anglican or Catholic, but few or none for Free Churches. David has already written a paper on worship trends that he has noticed over forty years down to 2005, appearing in the *Evangelical Quarterly* in 2007. There are two problems. The notes are written in tiny script; and they are in David's own shorthand for which, as we have seen, there is no written key. Apart from that, they give a clear picture of what actually goes on in services, something that David wishes so much had been left from the nineteenth century. He is able to trace changes in evangelical worship styles over nearly fifty years in the way they have affected the practice of communion, musical styles, the impact of technology—he has noticed, for example, that in many churches the "sound desk" provides an opportunity for male bonding, bringing together men with an interest in IT of all ages. He traces the change in the role of women and the different time weightings between preaching, praying, and singing. For the purposes of his 2007 paper, he drew on only a fraction of his notes and so there is plenty of scope for further writing in this field.

DAVID NOW

And so, what of David now? Very many of the early patterns are still there in his life. His mother's love of gathering information and David's very early desire to put it in order, his love of trips around the United Kingdom and now the world which he approaches with childlike excitement and zest, these both came from his earliest years. He had exposure to a very few books until eleven, but the few in his life made a huge impact on him. History came in with a bang with his Auntie Madge's Christmas present on his seventh birthday. The desire to write books on a global scale was there by nine. He always grew up knowing about Jesus and his Christian faith has developed deeply from the point of commitment when he was aged ten. The two main themes that are not major in his life now are heraldry and board games. He still loves them and has a cupboard of the latter, including Diplomacy, dreaded for its length, but he has rarely had time to play. This limitation has been largely the result of the ME because evenings are so short and he would find it hard to play in the daytime. Our granddaughter now enjoys Rummikub and The Game of Life and so maybe a revival of the old interest is imminent.

So what is his pattern day by day? He wakes far too early but always gets up at six no matter what. A lie-in is anathema to him. After walking to work (eighteen minutes past fields where rabbits play), he will be at work by 7:30 or so and thinks nothing of writing and researching until 12:45. He walks home, has lunch, and is back just after 2 for another four hours of work. He is amazingly well disciplined and ordered. Unless he has a conference, he normally works on Saturday mornings because of his school pattern. That can make it hard to achieve anything else because everything needs doing in the one afternoon of Saturday. What he still loves most is to plan a trip, to a castle or the coast or to our favorite small town of Crieff with its amazing fudge shop and Valentine's, the traditional men's outfitters—with, of course, a Chinese meal out in the evening, preferably at a new restaurant. He likes to have two weeks' holiday a year in a cottage or a bed and breakfast in a new part of the United Kingdom where he can explore new chapels and bookshops.

Sundays still have a busy rhythm with first an 8 a.m. Eucharist at the local Episcopal church and then the 9:45 service at Stirling Baptist Church with the 6:30 service in the evening. I meanwhile lead Lifeway, a Bible class for adults with learning disabilities, from 12:30 until 2 and join him at 9:45 and 6:30. On weekdays, once he has eaten in the evenings, there is not much time left, but usually he will fit in a DVD before he goes to bed at 9:00. *Hancock's Half Hour*, remembered from the 1960s, *Inspector Morse*, *After Henry* with its gentle bookshop settings, *Mapp and Lucia*, and David Suchet's wonderful *Poirot* series, these all give great pleasure.

So have we been compatible over the last forty-three years? In an amazing way, yes. I was brought up in a Nonconformist atmosphere in Northampton, that most Nonconformist of towns, primarily in a Congregational church but with Methodist and Baptist connections. My great-uncle was given the name Ewart after Gladstone and he was a Liberal councilor in Bournemouth. I was brought up having the letter box pointed out to me where Mr. G posted his letters while staying in Bournemouth. My grandmother had been close to P. T. Forsyth's daughter, Jessie, at Emmanuel Congregational Church in Cambridge in the late 1890s. I did A level history but then went on to read classics so I have always felt I knew enough of what David was writing about to be sternly critical but without competing with him in any way. In meticulous attention to detail we differ completely.

Footnotes irritate me and I never read them. Perhaps it is just as well that we are not both the same in this respect.

Eileen and David, Waco, Texas, 2011

The passion for book collecting has taken us to all sorts of lovely places, and when we are away, is part of David's forming a structure, which enables me to relax. I still enjoy pursuing my interests while he is browsing. We have noticed that by far the larger proportion of customers in secondhand bookshops consists of men. One thing I enjoy immensely about David is that his history gives him a broader perspective on life. For example, when we visit a new town or village, David is able to understand the historical and religious and often the political development of the area over the centuries just from what he sees. This is also true of current affairs. His long-standing interest in politics has developed to the point where he frequently has a deep understanding of the issues. He was long perturbed that Nagaland, the most Baptist region on earth, received no publicity at all even though it was under military occupation by the Indian armed forces—though happily a peace settlement now augurs more peaceful days for that remote part of northeast India. He can often make an illuminating comparison with events in earlier years. His understanding of theology, and especially of how history and theology mix, is second to none. I only wish he had more time to share more of it with others in an informal way.

    David has remained quite a simple person in his tastes and in some ways stays close to his Nottingham roots. He is never happier than with bacon sandwiches and an Ordnance Survey map exploring a new area, not empty country spaces but villages, towns, and cities. David always uses maps rather than sat-navs because he wants to see a place in its wider context. He remains urban by choice. He will briefly appreciate beautiful views in the countryside, but is keen to get back to buildings and people. We have been known to have our sandwiches on a traffic island in the middle of Bristol! He still loves to spend time in shops. After a long day of historical research he is delighted to pay a visit to a local supermarket as a reward. He does own a mobile / cell phone, but keeps it strictly for travel emergencies. He does not text on it or use iPhones or iPads. And he certainly does not use social networks. He finds it virtually impossible to read anyone's blog as he would much rather be reading a book. But he has embraced his Scottish heritage too and has been enriched by his years in Scotland. The height of fine dining to him would be a Chinese restaurant which is good value and has fast service. He hates waiting in restaurants. He has never intentionally drunk alcohol or smoked. He feels deeply grateful that his work, his hobby and his faith all intertwine. In fact it is almost impossible to know when he is working or not working, the links are so close. He likes to keep moving and exploring the intellectual worlds he is researching. He hates lines of all sorts. If in a traffic jam he would rather follow a nearby country route even if it takes much longer than sitting in a jam. Several times we have driven on small country roads around Catterick in Yorkshire because the A1 has been blocked. I personally would happily sit in the jam!

    So what of the future? Retirement is becoming a possibility, but David still loves teaching (usually!) and enjoys the company of his younger colleagues, and so that is an unknown at present. Computers are playing a larger and larger part in his life. Unlike some historians of his vintage who have spurned IT altogether, David is able to use it up to a point. He has a huge e-mail correspondence with the rest of the world and is often weighed down by enquiries of the "Please tell me all you know about . . ." sort. He is extremely supportive of younger scholars, or genuine scholars of any age. Technology may drive him to retirement in the end. He is now able to prepare powerpoints for lectures but is expected to retrieve them from his system and use them in the lecture theaters. He asks a colleague to help with this process and often it does not work for the assistant either. Being expected to perform operations he is not trained for depresses him.

He still has an insatiable thirst for understanding and truly reflects Socrates' definition of wisdom that he knew that he knew nothing. He usually expects everyone else to know more than he does. He has many ideas for books yet to write. Victorian Methodists in outlying areas of the British Isles are on the agenda and maybe a book on the similarities and differences between the United States and the United Kingdom. I would like him to write about how the major patterns of thought are reflected in Christian denominations. He still loves trips, especially across the world and approaches them with a strategy of finding out in advance as much as he can. He hates visiting the same place twice—which is hard on other people who like to revisit old haunts. He loves visiting other church services when away and becomes very frustrated if he cannot fit several in.

Books still feature very largely in his life. He returns to old favorites like *1066 and All That* from time to time. He loves his atlas given when he was six, especially the pages where it tells him how many days it takes to fly to far-flung places like Wellington, New Zealand (five and a half days!). *Winnie the Pooh* still delights him, as does *The Young Visiters* by the nine-year-old Daisy Ashford. He reads a huge variety of books. He has greatly valued literary suggestions from Jocelyn and the late Michael Charity of Cambridge who have enriched his reading both of humorous and serious literary works over the years. Recently he had by his bed a couple of modern novels, the published correspondence of Wagner and Nietzsche from the 1860s and 70s, a classic Faroese novel, and the biography of a distinguished historian, R. G. Collingwood. He regards all this as light reading! He has not moved into exploring e-books. So does he need his library? Could not all his books be found online? Some of them, yes, but certainly not all. The memoirs of obscure rural Nonconformists, which are his bread and butter, would not be obtainable in this way, besides which he likes direct access to the books. He does not want to be beholden to computers, batteries and chargers to access his information and this feeling stands apart from the pure enjoyment of physically handling the books. Also, when he is "gutting" many books in one morning, he needs to flick from page to page, perhaps back to retrieve a useful quotation, and this would take hours with

The Stirling Years

technology as it is at the moment. He simply could not work in the way he does at present with nothing but online resources, useful as they can be. When he cannot be reading, he is a devoted listener to the BBC Radio Four programs in the day and the BBC World Service through the long watches caused by his early waking. When in the United States he loves to find National Public Radio wherever he is.

Some modern trends make him sad and frustrated. He cares deeply about accurate grammar and punctuation to make sure communication is clear. And yet many students have not learned to write sentences that can be understood. Spelling mistakes on screens during church worship trouble him. Accuracy to him is honoring to God. The "utilitarian" view of the university which claims that its only purpose is to prepare people for jobs cuts across his belief in education as the development of humane attitudes and liberal values such as understanding and toleration. He is sad when the press condemns the public schoolboys who run the country because they come from the wealthy classes. They forget the scholarship boys such as David for whom education at a public school was provided because people believed in its value for itself. He is sad when money dictates policy decisions at the university, when the university library is reconstructed to make way for one with a smaller capacity and when academics in other departments regard books as things of the past. He shivers when he thinks of one Scottish university which has just knocked down the building containing the history department and has placed all the lecturers in open-plan offices where bookcases must not exceed waist high. He could not work in those conditions. He is sad when personal attention to students is minimized or when exclusively online marking is proposed. He is sad when he sees scientific method treated as the only possible way to approach knowledge when he knows that, in its present form, it is simply a post-Enlightenment phenomenon which displays some of the defects of its origins. He is sad when historians are obsessed with facts without ever reflecting about what facts actually are. He is sad when practitioners of other disciplines make assertions without backing up what they say with evidence.

So what is the legacy of all the history in his life? I would say "perspective." Items on the news rarely have the same effect on him as on other people because he will know that the same thing happened a hundred years ago or that there are similarities in another situation elsewhere that he knows about. His shorthand continues, as do his service notebooks. His life has very distinctive patterns in it still.

POSTSCRIPT

This story has added interest because it could not happen again in the same way. First, there is no longer an 11-plus exam in Nottingham and so the city would not fund its brightest boys to go to the High School. At Cambridge, David would not have a suite of rooms to himself and be encouraged to come up for a Long Vacation term when his role was just to read and study. There are no state scholarships to pay your fees and so graduates are burdened by huge debts. And the lifelong job at Stirling would probably have been impossible. Most young lecturers have to endure many short-term contracts before they obtain a tenured one. It is only in recent years that the Research Assessment Exercises and the REF exercise have come in, assessing everyone's research and causing enormous pressure to perform. David was free to pursue his own development. He feels grateful that he has served in higher education when he did. He will never stop learning and researching and hopefully writing as long as he has the strength. And who knows, one day he may write his own autobiography. Meantime, this book will give an insight into the patterns that have shaped his life and led to him tracing all sorts of patterns in history.

4
Conclusion

THESE THEN WERE THE steps by which the small boy from Nottingham came to be in Washington, DC, at New Year 2014. The very earliest traits can still be detected: the information gathering and the swift arranging into order; the old feeling that trips represent freedom from daily routine. His childhood fascination with adding to old patterns and forming new ones lives on. The Christian faith still forms a structure on which life is based. Charles Simeon's principle of "both . . . and" could apply to David himself. He is immersed in both history and geography and cannot separate the two. In his history he now works both on the macro level of huge worldwide waves of thought and on the micro level of how these played out in humble cottages in a nineteenth-century revival. He has become the legal professional that his mother so wanted him to be, but he has done it inside history, arguing a case for the new patterns he has formed and giving convincing evidence to back up his arguments. He has functioned as a forensic investigator, but within history, working from the clues of evidence to piece together what has been happening, often using evidence that no one else has thought of. He certainly has not let down the family expectations that he was to "do his own thing," not follow the crowd and be willing to be different. The Nottingham boy with the strong Scottish roots is clearly still to be seen in the present David. In an obituary for Reg Ward, another East Midlander who was one of David's role models, Jay Brown, Professor of Ecclesiastical History at Edinburgh and a good friend of David's, wrote that, though Ward was a productive historian, "he also remained firmly connected to his roots—Nonconformist, lower middle-class, teetotal, and provincial, with a strong Protestant work ethic and simple tastes." David too shares in this inheritance. His patterns have grown from similar roots.

APPENDIX 1

The Use of History

An address given, with variations,
to a wide range of audiences since 1979.

"HISTORY," ACCORDING TO HENRY Ford as reported in the *Chicago Tribune* for May 25, 1916, "is more or less bunk. It's tradition. We don't want tradition. We want to live in the present." Usually summarized as "History is bunk," the words of the hugely successful car manufacturer have resounded down the succeeding century. His opinion is widely shared. Only the present, with its boundless opportunities, counts; tradition, the legacy of the past, holds back humanity; history, its record, is useless. That point of view, however, is open to fundamental doubt. The past affects us in the present. Graffiti on walls in Northern Ireland sometimes say nothing but "1690." The date alone conveys a wealth of meaning. The year 1690 was the occasion of the battle of the Boyne, the victory of the Protestant William III over the Catholic James II. As a result there was a Protestant ascendancy in Ireland for over two centuries. To scrawl that date on a wall is to endorse the view that, in the north of Ireland that is still part of the United Kingdom, the Protestant community should remain dominant. We cannot escape from the legacy of the past by inhabiting the present, for the two are inextricably bound up together. Consequently the record of the past matters. History plays a crucial part in the human drama. A few of the more important reasons why it matters can be outlined here.

History provides, in the first place, a sense of identity. We say that something is wrong with people who have lost their memories and so we sympathize with them about what they lack. The same is true of nations or communities. Groups of people that lose their memories forfeit a sense of who they are and it is a cause for regret. A shared past, on the other hand, gives unity to any set of people. This principle is recognized in the United States, where American history is taught systematically in order to give citizens an awareness of their national identity. In Britain there have been powerful anxieties about low turnouts in successive elections to the European parliament. Participation in voting would be higher if there were a stronger consciousness of the links over the centuries between the countries of the island and of the continent. Thus, to take an example almost at random, the greatest German philosopher, G. W. F. Hegel, drew much of his economic thought from Sir James Steuart, a Scottish exile in Germany. The common heritage of Europe over the centuries binds its people together and the recollection of its dimensions should prompt a greater interest in its general welfare. A shared culture is crucial to any community. The memory of past heroes of the faith, as the cult of the saints has illustrated over the centuries, enriches the life of churches. That is true of Protestants as well as Catholics. For Baptists to forget William Carey or C. H. Spurgeon would be to abandon a large part of their corporate personality. Likewise in political societies a common web of allusions to the great names of the past, whether Abraham Lincoln or William Gladstone, helps gives a sense of the values of a nation. A sense of belonging, something virtually essential to human life, is provided by history.

A second benefit of history is an awareness of the background to public policy. The newspaper becomes a much more informative document if we possess a long view of the events that stand behind what it describes. Knowledge of how specific developments worked out their consequences in the past can profoundly deepen our grasp of the imperatives behind policy-making in our day. Thus the risks of inflation are powerfully illustrated by the fate of the Weimar Republic in Germany. This democratic constitutional system after the First World War was undermined by the runaway inflation of 1922–23 that eventually led to the American dollar being worth as many as 4,210,500,000,000 German marks. Apart from the sufferings of the people at the time from the worthlessness of their currency, the loss of life savings made many members of the middle classes desperate and so open to the blandishments of the far right. The rise to power of the Nazis in 1933 would hardly have been possible without the hyperinflation of a decade before. Those who framed economic strategy in later years had to take into account the disasters that ensued in the wake of a drastic reduction in the value of the German currency. Again the attitudes of foreign nations can hardly be grasped without an understanding of their past. Thus the policy of Israel on settlements in the West Bank, so detrimental to its image in the international world, is conditioned by the promises of territory in the Hebrew Bible. Because policy is so often molded by long-term factors, historians possess an advantage in public affairs. "History is past politics," observed E. A. Freeman in the late nineteenth century; "politics are present history." Although history now gives less exclusive priority to politics than in the past, historians do engage with issues of the exercise of power. That is no doubt why candidates for public office in many countries possess a background in the discipline of history. An awareness of policy questions in depth, however, is beneficial to a much wider section of the public. It is highly desirable in a democracy that the guidance and warning of past episodes should be available to as high a proportion of the population as possible. History performs a salutary function in helping an understanding of policy.

The discipline plays a role, thirdly, in dispelling prejudice. The word "history," as originally used by Herodotus, meant simply "inquiry." Historians inquire systematically, seeking truth. Consequently they call their own preconceptions as well as the assumptions of others into question. The outcome is often to demonstrate that alternative views of the past have merit. The Alsace-Lorraine question is a case in point. This territory was transferred from France to the new Germany in the wake of the Franco-Prussian War in 1871, returned to France after the First World War, reoccupied by Germany on the collapse of France in the Second World War but regained by France on its conclusion in 1945. Although most of the indicators of national identity pointed to the two provinces being French, they did possess features of German character too such as a significant Protestant population. A judicious historian would not wish to dismiss the German claims out of hand. Again, history can lay bare how claims can be simply wrong. The entrenched medieval belief that, by means of the Donation of Constantine, the emperor had transferred his authority in the West to the papacy was discredited when careful study in the fifteenth century revealed that the document was a forgery. History, furthermore, sets a question mark against some of the most cherished conventional beliefs of our age. It is common to suppose that religion and science are in constant conflict. A review of the history of the relationship between the two, however, would show that they have frequently been mutually supportive. In the early nineteenth century, for instance, there was a close integration between the two in what was called "natural theology," which framed the predominant way of looking at the world at the time. Religion has often been on the side of intellectual enquiry into the realm of nature. Deeper historical knowledge can undermine many of the mistaken opinions of the present day.

Nevertheless history, in the fourth place, enriches the quality of life in the present. The remains of the past, its material legacy in the built environment, surround us on every hand. They present us with a challenge, rather as the Himalayas presented a challenge to climbers, simply because they are there. They invite us to understand how they came to be and how they were deployed over the centuries. The late uncle of my wife, a successful bank manager, was rather suspicious of a historian joining the family. What use, he may have thought, was the newcomer's profession? Yet when the bank manager retired, he found that time hung heavy on his hands. He joined the National Trust that maintains historic buildings and spent much of each summer visiting its properties. He discovered the fascination of the inheritance of the present generation from the past. In many parts of the world the main tourist attractions are the sites of great events, spots associated with eminent writers or simply attractive structures from earlier ages. In Scotland the battlefield of Bannockburn recalls the struggles of the Middle Ages, the country home of Sir Walter Scott in the Borders reveals facets of his creative genius, and the city of Edinburgh, with its congested buildings in the Old Town and its stately terraces in the New Town, provides a magnificent case-study of an evolving townscape. In order to enjoy them to the full, a measure of historical expertise helps enormously. Thus to grasp the significance of Bannockburn some knowledge of heraldry and a grasp of the framework of a feudal society significantly enrich the experience of a visit. Yet even without much specialist understanding, a visitor can be stirred by the events commemorated at such sites. The heritage of the past is a dimension of history that can greatly enhance the informed use of leisure.

A fifth and final use of history is the training of the mind. History in its written form is not merely a story, for it requires argument to convince readers of its validity. The discipline trains its practitioners to argue a case. Not everybody has appreciated this dimension of the subject. Samuel Johnson, the eighteenth-century sage, supposed that history was markedly inferior to creative literature. "Great abilities," he once opined, "are not requisite for an Historian." The explanation, according to Johnson, was that the historian had so little to do. "He has the facts ready to his hand."

The Use of History

Stringing together facts might not require much capacity, but that is not what historians do. They have to assess the plausibility of evidence in order to decide what took place and to evaluate the relative importance of factors in determining outcomes. Such tasks demand intellectual skills of a high order. They are much like those displayed by able lawyers in court. Lawyers scrutinize evidence and weigh up probabilities in a similar way to historians—which is why so many successful lawyers come from a background of history. The written work of historians is comparable with the courtroom performances of the fictional Perry Mason, who characteristically puts forward a case built on fresh evidence to convince the jury that his client is innocent and that another person is the real murderer. Both engage in a rhetorical exercise to persuade their audience of the rightness of their contentions. Consequently historians, in acquiring their skills, gain habits of mind and techniques of analysis that are transferable to other spheres of life. The distinguished businessman Lord Sainsbury of Turville (b. 1940), who served as the chairman of one of the largest British supermarket chains and also as a government minister, had read history at Cambridge. In the process he learned, in his own words, "the ability to assimilate a mass of information, pull out of it the key issues and then produce coherent and persuasive arguments, on the basis of the evidence." Such a training of the mind is a key to success in any field of life.

History, then, is not bunk. We may want to live in the present, but the present is in continuity with the past. In order to understand the present, therefore, it is essential to understand the past. History is a tool for achieving that goal which has a variety of uses. It provides individuals, communities, and nations with a sense of identity. It supplies a means of comprehending political policies in depth. It enables people to overcome prejudice in themselves as well as in others. History allows us to enjoy a richer quality of life and the discipline provides distinctive intellectual skills. The subject is therefore not a diversion from the demands of contemporary life, but a craft that has a wide range of applications. Even Henry Ford came to appreciate something of the significance of history in his later years. During the 1920s he collected old buildings for historic villages and opened a museum of practical technology. Ford himself seems to have realized that history has its uses.

APPENDIX 2

William Wilberforce and Christian Duty

A sermon preached on Amos 5:4–15 at Holyrood Abbey Parish Church, Edinburgh, on March 25, 2007, the bicentenary of the passing of the abolition of the slave trade.

WILLIAM WILBERFORCE (1759–1833) IS known for leading the campaign for the abolition of the slave trade by an act of the UK Parliament passed on March 25, 1807. In the age of Napoleon, Britain was engaged in a struggle with France abroad. In an age of industrialization, there was rapid social change domestically. It was a period of dislocation in which injustice abounded. There was therefore a parallel with the time of the prophet Amos. In the eighth century BC, Amos denounced the abuse of power and compromise with ungodliness. Sections of chapter 5 of his prophecy relate to various aspects of Wilberforce's career. They can be taken for examination in turn.

1. VITAL RELIGION (VV. 4–6)

"Seek me and live" is the call of the Almighty to his people (vv. 4, 6). Knowing God personally is necessary for life. The people were not to go to Bethel, Gilgal or Beersheba, shrines where religious ceremonies took place. They were places of formal, outward religion. The people were not to seek that,

William Wilberforce and Christian Duty

for it would pass away under God's judgment. Rather they were to seek the Lord; they were to seek "vital religion."

That was Wilberforce's phrase for Evangelicalism. The movement, beginning in the 1730s, had reinvigorated Protestantism in the English-speaking world. It called for a special place for the Bible, the cross, conversion and activism. It gave fresh dynamic to the Church of Scotland under John Erskine of Edinburgh. Likewise it gave new vigor to the Church of England. Wilberforce was an Evangelical.

Born in the Yorkshire port of Hull, Wilberforce lost his father when he was eight years old. He was brought up by a grandfather, a prosperous merchant, who expected great things of his grandson. William proved successful at Hull Grammar School and then at St. John's College, Cambridge. He went on to be elected as Member of Parliament for Hull in 1780, when he was only twenty-one. Four years later he was returned as MP for Yorkshire, the largest county and the biggest constituency in the country, remaining in that position until 1812. At first he remained only a formal adherent of the Church of England, attending church regularly but treating it as an outward matter, much like the ritual of Bethel. In 1784–85, however, he undertook a continental tour with Isaac Milner, the brother of his former schoolmaster and an Evangelical clergyman. Together they read Philip Doddridge's *Rise and Progress of Religion in the Soul* and Wilberforce realized that "in the true sense of the word I was not a Christian." He submitted his life to the lordship of Christ, experiencing the "great change" of conversion. Should he, he asked himself, leave the hurly-burly of Parliament in order to seek peace outside? Consulting John Newton, the London Evangelical clergyman who was a former slave-ship captain and the author of the hymn "Amazing Grace," he was advised to remain at his post. A public career could be put at the service of Christ.

From that time onwards Wilberforce was active as an Evangelical. He tried to lead others to Christ, thinking up "launchers," conversational gambits to raise spiritual issues. He channeled all his natural qualities into the new path of discipleship. Possessing an abundance of charm and tact, he enjoyed male companionship, remaining a bachelor until he was thirty-eight years old. It was said that when he entered a room, sunshine would bathe the company. Yet he was a serious Christian, observing the feast days of the Church of England. He would put a pebble into his shoe in the morning as a reminder during the day that he was not to look for unalloyed happiness in this world. Wilberforce's religion was vital.

Because Wilberforce served in Parliament, he was able to defend the cause of the gospel there. In 1811 the spread of the Methodists across much of England caused alarm in the governing classes. Lord Sidmouth as Home Secretary intended to restrict their right to travel round the country as preachers, but Wilberforce successfully resisted the measure. Again in 1813 the charter of the East India Company that governed British India came up for revision. The company had previously excluded Christian missionaries from that land, but Wilberforce led a campaign in the House of Commons for a new clause in the charter providing that missionaries should enjoy freedom to preach the gospel in India. He was able to serve the Evangelical cause in Parliament.

Thus Wilberforce embraced vital Christianity. As a result he saw it as part of his duty to spread the gospel and to use his powers to defend the gospel.

2. PUBLIC JUSTICE (VV. 7-10)

Amos denounces any debasement of justice, turning it to bitterness (v. 7). He condemns hatred for an individual who speaks the truth in court, simply upholding right standards (v. 10). Those who are not committed to justice ignore the Almighty, but God cannot be safely ignored. The Lord is the creator, who can also bring destruction in the world (vv. 8, 9). Therefore his standards should not be forgotten in public affairs. There must be a commitment to public justice.

Wilberforce as a Christian politician felt he had to assume the role of an assertor of that principle. He wrote to a constituent in 1789: "A man who acts from the principles I profess reflects that he is to give an account of his political conduct at the Judgement Seat of Christ." His responsibility was the promotion of righteousness in the public arena. Wilberforce was not wholly successful, for he suffered from flaws of character. Like many warm-hearted people, he was too easygoing. He would leave important letters unanswered for months. He was therefore judged wholly unfit for public office. There was never any question of Wilberforce being in government.

Yet he did try to establish higher standards in national life. The eighteenth century had a plethora of legislation encouraging good behavior among the mass of the population. There were laws against blasphemy, drunkenness, and Sabbath desecration. The problem was that justices of the peace failed to enforce these measures in the localities. If the nation was to be more righteous, the rules would need to be put into practice. Therefore Wilberforce launched a campaign for what was called the "reformation of manners." It helped that an old friend from college, William Pitt, was Prime Minister, with only a short break, from 1784 to 1806. Wilberforce secured support for his campaign from Pitt, who in turn persuaded the king to issue, in 1787, a proclamation urging justices of the peace to implement the existing legislation. Wilberforce followed up this success by encouraging the creation of local Proclamation Societies, groups designed to prod reluctant justices into action. As a result many in the population thought twice about unseemly behavior.

Increasingly Wilberforce cooperated with a circle of friends who were mostly Evangelicals. Living chiefly in the leafy London suburb of Clapham, they have been dubbed by historians the "Clapham Sect." They included able men such as the banker and MP Henry Thornton and the lawyer James Stephen, who became Wilberforce's brother-in-law. They acted together over the years to push forward a large number of measures. Usually in concert with this group, Wilberforce took up a variety of causes: prison reform, urging more and better prison accommodation; the end of hanging, which Wilberforce considered "a barbarous mode" of execution; and, in his later years, the extension of full civil rights to Roman Catholics, an illustration that the Claphamites believed in religious liberty not just for themselves but for all.

Consequently Wilberforce became a prominent public figure in a variety of causes. His method was important: he did not act like many Evangelicals, making peremptory demands and rousing loud agitations. Rather, he was flexible in his tactics. There was, he observed, "room for consideration of times and seasons." Sometimes an issue should be pressed, but at other times it should be held back. Here was a type of political shrewdness that was better calculated to achieve results than constant clamor. It is probably significant that he was a politician before he was an Evangelical, so that a recognition of the constraints and limitations of political power came more naturally to him.

Wilberforce, then, pursued high standards in national policy. He showed wisdom in his quest for political justice.

3. DEFENSE OF THE WEAK (VV. 11–12A)

Amos addresses the well-to-do, those who build stone mansions and plant lush vineyards (v. 11). They were trampling on the poor, making the weak their victims. In particular, the prosperous folk were exploiting the poor by forcing them to hand over their grain. Humble working people were not allowed keep the fruit of their own labor. Amos condemns this activity as sinful.

Wilberforce encountered similar circumstances in the slave trade. Slaves were the ultimate in weakness, being treated as subhuman. Their labor was exploited mercilessly. The trade in slaves was the focus of Wilberforce's attention. During the eighteenth century there was a three-way trade across the Atlantic. Vessels took British exports to Africa; there they loaded victims of African wars, carrying them in the so-called middle passage across the ocean to the slave plantations of the Caribbean and North America; and then the ships returned with the products of the plantations to Britain. There were appalling conditions on board during the middle passage. One man could be manacled to a corpse in the hold; notoriously in a storm, the ship might be lightened by throwing slaves overboard; and about one-fifth of the slaves were normally so ill on their arrival that they were treated as refuse. The slave trade enriched the merchants, but it was utterly inhuman.

Why was it abolished in 1807? The explanation, according to some historians, is economic self-interest. The trade, on this interpretation, was ceasing to be profitable and so could safely be surrendered. It has been shown, however, that such an understanding cannot be sustained. Although profits from the slave trade were lower by 1807 than they had been previously, it still provided a solid source of income. The causes of abolition have to be located elsewhere. The change came about partly because of the intellectual atmosphere of the Enlightenment. Increasingly the eighteenth century saw liberty, happiness, and benevolence as ideals to be implemented, but the slave trade infringed them all. Public opinion was steadily turning against the trade. Undoubtedly, however, the Evangelicals were the shock troops of the campaign, bringing their characteristic energy into the efforts for ending the trade. The reason is that they had become convinced that the trade was sinful. As Wilberforce put it, "When the actual commission of guilt is in question, a man who fears God is not at liberty." Accordingly Wilberforce threw himself into the cause. He first proposed resolutions in the House of Commons against the slave trade in 1789. They did not carry, and there was merely an agreement to assemble evidence, an enterprise at which Wilberforce and his friends excelled. He proposed further resolutions against the trade over the years, but faced dogged resistance from the West India merchants. The well-to-do gentry who dominated the Commons thought abolition a very radical proposal. It was a long struggle.

The campaign came to a head in 1806–07. In 1806 the Evangelicals in the Commons successfully argued that, because of the conditions of the war against Napoleon, there should be partial suspension of the trade. In 1807 they argued from the precedent of the previous year that there should be total abolition. A sympathetic government was in office and the measure carried. It was an instance of skilful parliamentary tactics, not just airy idealism, giving the members of the Clapham sect a buoyant sense of victory. After the second reading of the abolition bill, Wilberforce asked Henry Thornton, "Well, Henry, what should we abolish next?"

Wilberforce took upon himself the championship of the least powerful group in the contemporary world, the victims of the slave trade. He was a defender of the weak.

4. COURAGEOUS STATEMENT (VV. 12B–13)

Amos shows courage. He denounces the unjust to their faces, addressing them directly as "you," and censuring them even though they are powerful. Those in charge were oppressive, took bribes, and deprived the poor of justice (v. 12b). In such wicked times, those guided only by prudent self-interest would keep quiet (v. 13). Amos, however, does not remain silent, but speaks out despite the risks.

Likewise Wilberforce spoke out in the circumstances of his time. He did not just champion political causes, but set out his convictions in print. In 1797 he published *A Practical View of the Prevailing Religious System of Professed Christians*. Directed to the "higher and middle classes," it condemned the normal religious profession of a gentleman, the veneer of belief needed to sustain respectability that was compatible with dueling, gambling, and theater-going. Wilberforce insisted, on the contrary, that faith is to mold the whole of life, requiring vital religion and its high moral standards. The book proved highly successful, selling 7,500 copies within six months and often being reprinted.

It is crucial to stress that, like Amos, Wilberforce was addressing those who were in charge, not the bulk of the population. Wilberforce's career, in the view of some historians, was essentially about keeping the lower classes in order. That, after all, was the thrust of the campaign for the reformation of manners. In the wake of the French Revolution, on this reading of events, the British ruling classes wanted to prevent the masses from abandoning their place at the base of the social pyramid. Wilberforce, according to this school of opinion, was assisting the exercise of social control. How valid is this point of view? It is true that Wilberforce believed that the lower orders should remain in their station and that the established constitution should be respected. He made a point of speaking in favor of every law designed to uphold public order passed between 1795 and 1819. Nevertheless his book *A Practical View* shows that such a historical case is mistaken. He certainly believed that the mass of the people must observe Christian standards, but he also held that the higher classes were bound to do the same. Christian principles applied to all ranks of society.

So Wilberforce set down his views about the wickedness of the powerful. He made a courageous effort to point out to them the need to change their ways.

5. PERSISTENT GOODNESS (VV. 14, 15)

"Seek good," declares Amos, "not evil" (v. 14). Then he reverses the challenge: "Hate evil, love good" (v. 15). God, he assures the people, will in that case be with them and have mercy. So his hearers were to pursue goodness, persevering in the task. They were to "maintain justice" (v. 15), not just once but consistently.

Wilberforce did not rest content with the abolition of the slave trade in 1807. He persevered in his concern for the slaves. He ensured the enforcement of abolition, prodding the government into deploying naval squadrons to intercept vessels still carrying slaves even though the practice was now illegal. In 1814 he organized a mass petition to Parliament, signed by nearly a million individuals, calling for the effective suppression of the trade. He also pressed for international abolition. Denmark had ended the trade in 1803 and the United States followed in 1808, but most European countries still permitted it. Wilberforce stirred up British pressure on them to suppress it. In 1814, again, he tried to incorporate the abolition of the slave trade in the peace treaty with France. And he urged measures for the amelioration of the condition of the slaves on the plantations. That was to move beyond the trade to the institution of slavery itself. Wilberforce

William Wilberforce and Christian Duty

hoped for the gradual emancipation of all the slaves in British dominions. In 1823 the Commons resolved in favor of gradual emancipation, though at that stage the decision was only an expression of principle. Yet Wilberforce was making progress on behalf of the slaves because of his sustained commitment.

Wilberforce was not actively involved in the eventual solution of the problem of slavery in British territory. In 1825, when well into his sixties, Wilberforce left Parliament. The campaign on behalf of the slaves continued, now led by Thomas Fowell Buxton, another Evangelical. Then events quickened for three reasons. For one thing, the Evangelical public at large became convinced that slavery was intrinsically wicked. Slave owners started restricting missionaries on their plantations and so became opponents of the gospel. Since slavery had become intolerable, Evangelicals demanded not gradual emancipation, Wilberforce's view, but immediate emancipation. Slaves, in the second place, played a part in affairs. In 1831 roughly 40 percent of the slaves in Jamaica rose in rebellion against their masters. Although the insurrection was suppressed, it became clear that it would be hard to keep the slaves in subjection for an indefinite period. Thirdly, Parliament was reformed. After the Great Reform Act of 1832, the much larger electorate contained many voters of Evangelical conviction. At the general election of the same year, they demanded that candidates would pledge themselves to support the termination of slavery.

As a result, in 1833 Parliament voted for the ending of slavery in British dominions, which came fully into force in 1838. Wilberforce heard the news of the parliamentary decision three days before he died. Even if he was not responsible for the eventual emancipation of the slaves, he had persisted in his campaign on their behalf. He had hated evil and loved good.

CONCLUSION

What, then, does Wilberforce show about Christian duty? He was a specialist, giving time to important causes, especially the abolition of the slave trade. Because he specialized, he could collect evidence, create networks, and plan tactics. Christians need such experts to participate in public affairs, to take up a cause, and to enter the legislature. Not every believer is expected to play this sort of part, but some are called to it. For all of us, however, Wilberforce points to Christian duties. We do well to bear them in mind. All Christians are to illustrate the qualities called for by Amos and embodied in Wilberforce. There is vital religion. We are to embrace the gospel and defend its interests. There is public justice. We are to look for high standards in political policies. There is defense of the weak. We are to care first of all for the needy and oppressed. There is courageous statement. We are to be prepared to set out the responsibilities of those in higher places. And there is persistent goodness. We are not just to endorse simple goodness, but to persevere in it ourselves. In our own spheres, whatever they may be, are these the values for which we stand? Wilberforce did, and so can we.

APPENDIX 3

The Christian Scholar and the Scriptures
A sermon preached on Psalm 119:41–48 at Liberty University, Lynchburg, Virginia, on September 28, 2011, and at Oak Hill College, London, on January 12, 2012.

Psalm 119 is the longest of the psalms and so this sermon is confined to exploring one section of it. The Psalm is divided into strophes, each of which contains eight verses starting with the same letter, going through the Hebrew alphabet from *aleph* to *taw*. Verses 41–48 consist of the strophe starting with *waw*. That posed a problem for the psalmist, since very few words in Hebrew begin with that letter. His solution was to use *waw* as a conjunction meaning "so" or "and" at the beginning of each line. That is why "so" or "and" appear several times at the start of lines in the King James Version of the Bible. The passage we are going to examine is therefore something of a triumph of literary ingenuity.

The message of the whole psalm is about the law of God. There are ten synonyms for "law," at least one in every verse, within this strophe. They appear as the terms "promise," "word" and so on as well as "law." They are mostly interchangeable, all of them referring to God's revealed and written will. For the Christian, that is to be found in the Scriptures. The psalm is therefore rightly understood as being about the Bible.

We are studying this psalm in a Christian college. We therefore concern ourselves not only with what this passage says to us as believers, but also with its significance for us as a community of students. We are

Christian learners and teachers, in some way Christian scholars. What do verses 41–48 have to tell us in that capacity? What are the marks of the Christian scholar according to the Scriptures?

1. GRACE (V. 41)

"May your unfailing love come to me." The psalmist requests "unfailing love" or "mercies" (KJB), the Hebrew word *hesed* in the plural. That is the Old Testament equivalent of the New Testament "grace," undeserved, faithful love. The request is offered to the "LORD," which is Yahweh, the personal name of God; and it is made on behalf of "me," the individual personally. So a personal reception of grace is sought from its source. The parallel expression in the second half of the verse, "salvation," shows that the grace is designed to deliver us from all that ensnares us. It is offered "according to your word," in harmony with what God has promised us in his revelation.

Therefore the first mark of the Christian scholar is to seek grace, to enter the salvation that God offers, to become a Christian. It follows that we are not to seek wisdom first. We may compare a passage in the New Testament. "Where is the scholar?" asks Paul in 1 Corinthians 1:20. "Has not God," he goes on, "made foolish the wisdom of the world?" The wisdom derived from the world is worth nothing, for true wisdom lies in Christ crucified (v. 23). Like all human beings, therefore, we are first to seek salvation by grace through the work of Christ upon the cross.

The life of John Wesley illustrates the point. Wesley was a scholar, a fellow of Lincoln College, Oxford, in the 1730s. He read extremely widely, as we know from his surviving booklists, in his quest for wisdom. Yet, because he possessed no experience of Christ crucified, the knowledge he accumulated meant very little. That changed on May 24, 1738, the day Wesley's heart was "strangely warmed" as he believed personally in Christ. Only then did his scholarship ignite into forceful preaching and Methodism was born. Wesley reminds us that, as the book of Proverbs declares repeatedly, the fear of the Lord is the beginning of wisdom. The fear of the Lord is not the culmination of a long quest, as mystics of many traditions have supposed; nor is it picked up on the way, as many broad-minded Protestants have hoped. Rather the fear of the Lord is the beginning of wisdom.

The current Dissenting Academies Project in which I am involved is examining the eighteenth- and nineteenth-century institutions that trained men for the ministry among English Nonconformists. The Evangelical colleges always made what they called "piety" a condition of entry. They looked for signs that anybody enrolled in their ranks was converted. Without piety, they recognized, learning was worthless in the ministry. Preachers of the gospel initially needed the gospel themselves.

So it is with scholars. If we are to serve Christ, we have to possess authentic piety. We need to have trusted Christ's "unfailing love." Christian scholars are to be Christian.

2. APOLOGETICS

Then, continues the psalmist, "I will answer the one who taunts me." All believers are open to taunts, and so anyone may give an answer. For the Christian scholar, however, particular taunts are likely. They are the criticisms mounted by sceptics, in the nineteenth century by freethinkers, and in the twenty-first century by unashamed atheists such as Richard Dawkins. We have to appreciate that there is a contest of ideas in Western civilization between faith and shades of unbelief. It is extremely valuable if our scholarship can contribute not just to the advance of knowledge but also to the defense of the faith, to apologetics. Each of us can usefully be what British coins declare the queen to be: "Fid. Def.," *Fidei Defensor*, a defender of the faith.

How can that best be done? According to verse 42, we can "trust in your word." Good apologetic is not counter-taunts, railing against opponents, denunciation, but sober explanation of biblical reasons for believing together with peaceable standards of statement. It can be achieved ingeniously. A good example is the work by Timothy Larsen of Wheaton College, Illinois, called *A People of One Book* (2011). It shows that in Victorian Britain, all strands of opinion respected the Bible. It was not just Evangelicals who placed great value on the Scriptures but also others such as E. B. Pusey, the High Churchman, and even Charles Bradlaugh, the secularist. The book is good history but also good apologetic, implying that if such figures possessed that degree of esteem for the Bible, so should likeminded individuals today.

There can be less exalted techniques of apologetic work such as holding a meeting after the evening service for young people where a recent book is scrutinized from a Christian angle by a specialist in the field. The power of apologetic is nowhere better demonstrated, however, than by C. S. Lewis, the Oxford scholar of medieval and early modern literature. His radio presentations on basic Christian doctrine, *Broadcast Talks* (1942), reprinted in *Mere Christianity*, form a classic of the art. They are well worth imitating in our day, though with the proviso that new studies should engage with up-to-date issues. A contemporary text in the field should, for example, deal with questions raised by postmodernism.

Christian scholars, then, have an opportunity to reply to those who taunt them and other believers. Trusting in the word of the Lord, they can mount a powerful apologetic. Christian scholars are to provide answers.

3. COMMUNICATION (V. 43)

The psalmist asks the Almighty not to snatch the word of truth from his mouth. He does not want to have the words taken away from his lips: he wants to be allowed to communicate. That should always be the prayer of the Christian scholar: a plea to be allowed to pass on the true knowledge that he or she has acquired. There is a desire to transmit knowledge, to teach.

The reason given is that the psalmist has put his hope in God's "laws." Here, unusually, the word translated "laws" is probably significant. It is not a word for law overall, but a term for *ad hoc* decisions, for verdicts, for the application of law in general to particular situations. The subject is how the will of the Almighty relates to the detail of life: it is about God's "apps." The psalmist is confident that the divine purpose can be put into operation in this way. The word of truth that the Christian scholar communicates is to be practical, to be applied to life.

A good instance of how that principle can work out in practice is the Baylor Institute for the Study of Religion, a part of Baylor University, Texas. This social scientific organization is thoroughly academic, but also practice-related. It shows how Christianity produces benefits in society. A large-scale statistical survey under its auspices, for example, has demonstrated that faith is a factor making for greater health. That is the sort of knowledge that the Christian scholar is to hand on. Commonly the transmission will not be through research institutes but through the simple medium of teaching. The next generation can be shown the advantages accruing to society through the Christian faith. That does not mean obscuring the blots on the Christian record, which must be as faithfully chronicled as in the Bible, but it does mean revealing the role of Christianity as a force for good in the community.

The Christian Scholar and the Scriptures

The classic text about university education, John Henry Newman's book *The Idea of a University* (1873), enquires about the purpose of a university. The answer is that a university exist "to teach universal knowledge." That formula, though conceived before research became integral to higher education, is not a bad one. It proposes that universities are to further knowledge rather than just engage in speculation; they are to inculcate all branches of knowledge, not just a narrow part of it; and they are to teach it, to pass it on. Christian scholars want to perform that function. They do not want the word of truth to be taken out of their mouth.

Christian scholars are in the business of communication. They believe their calling is the transmission of knowledge.

4. OBEDIENCE (V. 44)

"I will always obey your law," declares the psalmist. Christians, that is to say, are under a moral obligation. That needs stating because some Christians suppose that they are above the moral law. There is a risk of antinomianism, the claim that since we are under grace, we are not obliged to keep the law of God. The truth, however, is the reverse. If we have received grace, we are under the greater obligation to keep the law from the motive of gratitude. We are not free from the law.

There is perhaps a special snare here for the academic. It is sometimes easy to see the self-interested reasons why some people keep the law and to feel that, in view of the hypocrisy they display, there is no reason to make an effort to obey the divine directions. But the psalmist insists that he wants to keep the law "always," "for ever and ever." It is not a case of "usually" or "in general." The Christian should surely be scrupulous about obedience.

One example relates to future plans, which those carving out academic careers often formulate in some detail. We have to recognize that any plans of ours are wholly dependent on what the Lord has in store for us. For that reason Christians often used to say that they would do such and such "D. V.," *Deo volente*, if God wills. The phrase has been largely dropped, no doubt rightly, because of its archaic sound. Yet it expresses the truth that we must not assume that the future is ours to mold. James 4:13–15 teaches that we are not to say we shall go to some city and make money. Instead we should say, "if it is the Lord's will" we shall go. We can therefore say that we "hope" to undertake some research project, not that we "shall" do it. Careful language about our intentions is a good instance of trying to be alert to keep God's law "always."

Christian scholars have a variety of particular temptations about observing divine commands. Speakers at conferences may be lured towards increasing their travel expenses a little. Natural scientists may be snared into making laboratory results fit the desired outcomes more than they do. All of us may be inclined to feel censorious about other Christians who do not understand issues as well as we suppose we do. A host of pitfalls is waiting for us. So we need to resolve to obey the commands of the Lord "for ever and ever."

Christian scholars are not above the law of God. They have the responsibility of obedience.

5. FREEDOM (V. 45)

The psalmist tells us that he will "walk about in freedom." The idea is literally that he will take a stroll "in a broad space." He is not confined, limited or oppressed. Rather, he delights in the liberty he enjoys.

It is, however, a common idea that Christians are cramped because of their faith. A book that I reviewed on the literature of Nonconformist Wales discusses the many Welsh authors of the twentieth century who saw its chapels as sources of the repression of the national psyche, binding the people with inhibitions. Dylan Thomas, the Welsh poet, writes of the gloom of the "tin Bethels." The book itself reinforces the message by its title: *In the Shadow of the Pulpit*. Christianity is often censured for such repression.

Surely, however, Christian scholars can help wipe away that reproach. They can show that Christian practice has a paradox at its heart. Freedom comes through submission to Christ. As Jesus himself put it, "If the Son makes you free, you will be free indeed" (John 8:36). In verse 45 of the psalm, liberty is associated with seeking out God's precepts. Acknowledging our obligation to the Almighty makes us free. Augustine's principle of ethics is, "Love and do what you will." If we truly love, we are free to behave in accordance with our own wills. So a root Christian allegiance actually fosters liberty.

Christian scholars can put that axiom into practice. They are free for cultural creativity. The Puritans, so often denounced for their narrowness, were in reality extraordinarily capable of imaginative triumphs. Samuel Rutherford, a great Scottish theologian of the seventeenth century, boldly applied the language of marriage to the relation of the soul to its Redeemer. John Bunyan deployed the idea of pilgrimage, though it was then condemned as a Catholic error, to compose a Christian allegory that has exercised a fascination over readers ever since. In these cases the ideas of the faith have enriched rather than impoverished literature. Christian scholars can aspire to do the same.

The freedom enjoyed by all believers has special significance for Christian scholars. Enjoying a sense of liberty themselves, they can demonstrate that Christianity is no oppressive creed.

6. CONFIDENCE (V. 46)

"I will speak of your statutes before kings," announces the psalmist. He expresses fearless confidence. At a time when kings held arbitrary powers, he would testify to God's truth before them. He would not be put to shame in their presence.

This code of action has at times been adopted by Christians. Quakers in particular have a tradition of testifying to the authorities. In the nineteenth century, members of their society travelled to Russia to call upon the czar to treat his peasantry with greater justice. Here was a telling instance of speaking truth to power. More recently Billy Graham has acted as a trusted counselor to successive presidents of the United States. In these and other cases, Christians have talked about what the psalmist calls God's "statutes," his principles for policy. They were drawing the attention of those in power to the divine perspective on life.

For Christian scholars, the verse applies primarily to a different category of authorities. They are accountable not to kings but to academic opinion. Can we speak about a divine perspective in that context? Yes: surely it is the calling of the Christian scholar to bring together faith and learning, to explore how particular disciplines fit into a Christian worldview. That, according to the historian George Marsden, is the "outrageous idea" of Christian scholarship.

In the early and middle years of the twentieth century, academic authorities did tend to see committed scholarship of this kind as outrageous. It was generally supposed that all disciplines should be marked by academic objectivity. That axiom was interpreted to mean that any linking of scholarship to faith was to contaminate it. It was hard to perform academic work Christianly. In our day, however, that understanding of objectivity has been largely superseded. It is generally accepted that scholars cannot avoid points of view. As a result a Christian perspective has become more admissible. A few academic rulers may still raise an eyebrow, but the idea of applying Christian categories to research projects has become much less outlandish than it was. Christian scholars may pursue distinctively Christian scholarship more freely. That makes what would in any case be our calling a far more practicable venture than in the recent past.

It is a Christian virtue to speak out about a divine perspective on life to those in authority. For Christian scholars that entails not being ashamed of their distinctive perspective.

7. DELIGHT (V. 47)

The psalmist will delight in the commands of God. Any believer is not to see obeying God's revelation as onerous, a matter of grudging conformity. Rather, he or she is to delight in the divine commands, relishing the Bible as their source. We should expect to see wonderful things in God's law (Psalm 119:18). When I am asked my favorite verse in the Bible, I sometimes answer that it is Ecclesiastes 10:11: "If the snake bites before it is charmed, there is no advantage in a charmer" (NRSV). At first it seems an extraordinary thought to find a place in revelation, but the verse vividly brings out the rooting of the book of which it is a part in the Middle East. That is the sort of wonderful thing that can elicit delight.

The delight is possible because of love. The psalmist goes on to say that he loves God's commands. As Jesus put it, where our treasure is, there our heart will be also (Matt 6:21). If we find the Bible a treasure-house, we shall love it. That will enhance our pleasure in its contents in all their variety.

Christian scholars, however, will want to let their delight in the Scriptures operate in a specific way. They will want to allow biblical passages to illuminate not just their lives but their work. Michael Faraday, the great nineteenth-century English scientist who specialized in electromagnetism, certainly allowed his Christian faith to impinge on his science. When asked in the Crimean War to advise about chemical weapons, for example, he refused to assist what he considered immoral methods of warfare. But his faith went deeper into the content of his science than that. Faraday was a member of the Sandemanians, a small sect of Scottish origins with distinctively rational views on biblical interpretation. It has been shown that Faraday used the same methods for understanding Scripture and for investigating the world. His discoveries were the fruit of his love of the Bible. Faraday is an exemplar for Christian scholars.

All believers are to delight in God's revelation. Christian scholars, however, are particularly called to relish the Bible.

8. MEDITATION (V. 48)

The final verse of the strophe tells of lifting up hands to the commands of the Lord. The raising of the hands, as the customary posture of prayer in the ancient world, was a gesture of reverence. Hence the New Revised Standard Version translates the line "revere." The psalmist is commending high respect for the commands of God, which, as he repeats, he loves. But he goes further. It is possible to revere the Bible without applying it to oneself. It is possible to assert the importance of biblicism without exploring its significance in detail. That is not what the psalmist wants. Instead he writes of meditating on the divine decrees.

Meditation on the Bible is a valuable practice. It means lingering over a verse or even a word, revolving it in the mind and probing its implications. The practice can be undertaken at night, which is helpful since those of scholarly disposition often suffer from insomnia. Or it can be a daytime activity. It is possible to choose a verse and return to it on several occasions during the day, seeking new meaning each time. Meditation is characteristically open-ended, making fresh connections. It is a pondering of spiritual things.

The result is a storing up of theological knowledge, a putting the teachings of Scripture into order. That should be the goal of every Christian scholar. It is not enough to display skill in an academic discipline. If we believe in a combination of faith and learning, we need a structured grasp of both. It is good that there are professional theologians, but every Christian scholar has a calling to be an amateur theologian.

In the process of building up our own theological convictions, it is crucial that we do not twist Scripture to our own ends. The scholars at work on the King James Bible, for all their skills, were required by royal instruction to translate the word "*ecclesia*" not as "congregation," a natural rendering, but as "church." The aim was to bolster the claims of the state church, which was effectively done.

Christian scholars today may be under less political pressure to interpret Scripture in a particular way (though in some lands the pressures remain very similar). There may, however, be subtler pressures. Personal preferences or a desire to conform may lead us to lean towards a particular interpretation of the Bible. For that reason sustained meditation is vital. We need to work out the real meaning of Scripture in depth. That will enrich our thinking and writing as well as our lives.

So it emerges that Christian scholars do well to spend time in reflection on Scripture in an open-ended way. Like the psalmist, we can meditate on God's decrees.

CONCLUSION

In exploring the theme of the Christian scholar and the Scriptures, we have discovered a number of points. First there is grace: the Christian scholar must be a Christian. Then there is apologetics: the Christian scholar should be ready with an answer. Communication is important: the Christian scholar will want to transmit knowledge. Obedience is also crucial: the Christian scholar is to keep the law. The outcome is freedom: the Christian scholar is to enjoy liberty. There is confidence: the Christian scholar will not be ashamed of a distinctive perspective. Delight follows: the Christian scholar can relish the Bible. And meditation is productive: the Christian scholar will want to ponder the Scriptures. If our scholarship bears those marks, it will be truly Christian. Then it will serve the purposes of our master, Jesus Christ.

APPENDIX 4

Curriculum Vitae of David Bebbington

Born Nottingham, July 25, 1949

Attended Seely Primary School, Sherwood, Nottingham, 1954–60

Attended Nottingham High School, 1960–68

Exhibitioner of Jesus College, Cambridge, 1968–70

    Historical Tripos: Part I, 1970: Class I

Scholar of Jesus College, Cambridge, 1970–71

    Historical Tripos: Part II, 1971: Class I

    BA, 1971 (MA, 1974)

Research Student at Jesus College, Cambridge, 1971–73

    Baptist Historical Society prize, 1972

Research Fellow of Fitzwilliam College, Cambridge, 1973–76

    Hulsean Prize in Ecclesiastical History (of the university), 1973

    PhD, 1975

Lecturer in History, University of Stirling, 1976–89

    Trustees' Lectures at Union Theological College, Belfast, 1980

    Laing Lecture at London Bible College, 1982

    Fellow of the Royal Historical Society, 1986

Senior Lecturer in History, University of Stirling, 1989–91

    Visiting Professor, Department of History, University of Alabama, Birmingham, 1990

Reader in History, University of Stirling, 1991–99

Curriculum Vitae of David Bebbington

    Visiting Professor, Regent College, Vancouver, 1992

    Visiting Professor, Graduate School, Notre Dame University, Indiana, 1994

    Visiting Professor, Faculty of Theology, University of Pretoria, 1995

    Ben Marais Lecture at the University of Pretoria, 1995

    Hayward Lectures at Acadia Divinity School, Nova Scotia, 1998

Professor of History, University of Stirling, 1999–present

    Didsbury Lectures at the Nazarene Theological College, Manchester, 1999

    Drew Lecture at Spurgeon's College, London, 2000

    Fellow of St Deiniol's Library, Hawarden, 2002

    Visiting Distinguished Professor, Department of History, Baylor University, Texas, 2003, 2005, 2007, 2009 and 2011

    Finlayson Lecture of the Scottish Evangelical Theology Society, Edinburgh, 2004

    Murray Lecture at Atlantic Baptist University, Moncton, New Brunswick, 2004

    Willson-Aldis Lecture at Truett Seminary, Baylor University, Texas, 2005

    Laing Lecture at the London School of Theology, 2006

    Branson Lecture at Burleigh College, Adelaide, 2006

    S. R. Gardiner Lecture at the Sevenoaks Historical Society, Kent, 2006

    President, Ecclesiastical History Society, 2006–07

    Oklahoma Baptist University Centennial Commemoration Lecture, 2007

    Hughey Lectures at the International Baptist Theological Seminary, Prague, 2008

    Charles Perry Lecture at Ridley College, Melbourne, 2009

    Deere Lectures at Golden Gate Baptist Theological Seminary, San Francisco, 2009

    Friends of Dr Williams's Library, London, Annual Lecture, 2010

    Fellow of the Ecclesiastical History Society, 2011

    Moule Lecture at Ridley Hall, Cambridge, 2012

APPENDIX 5

Books Published by David Bebbington

A History of Queensberry Street Baptist Church, Old Basford, Nottingham. Nottingham, 1977.
Patterns in History. Leicester: InterVarsity; Downers Grove: InterVarsity, 1979. Rev. ed., *Patterns in History: A Christian Perspective on Historical Thought*. Grand Rapids: Baker, 1990; Leicester: InterVarsity, 1991. 3rd ed., Vancouver: Regent College, 2001. Korean ed., Seoul: InterVarsity, 1997.
The Nonconformist Conscience: Chapel and Politics, 1870–1914. London: Allen & Unwin, 1982. 2nd ed., London: Routledge, 2010.
The Baptists in Scotland: A History (edited). Glasgow: Baptist Union of Scotland, 1988.
Evangelicalism in Modern Britain: A History from the 1730s to the 1980s. London: Unwin Hyman, 1989. Rev. ed., Grand Rapids: Baker, 1992; London: Routledge, 1993. Korean ed., Seoul: InterVarsity, 1998.
Victorian Nonconformity. Bangor, Gwynedd: Headstart History, 1992. Rev. ed., Eugene, Oregon: Wipf & Stock; Cambridge: Lutterworth, 2011.
William Ewart Gladstone: Faith and Politics in Victorian Britain. Grand Rapids: Eerdmans, 1993.
Evangelicalism: Comparative Studies of Popular Protestantism in North America, the British Isles, and Beyond, 1700–1990 (coedited with Mark Noll and George Rawlyk). New York: Oxford University Press, 1994.
Holiness in Nineteenth-Century England. Carlisle: Paternoster, 2000.
Gladstone Centenary Essays (coedited with Roger Swift). Liverpool: Liverpool University Press, 2000.
The Gospel in the World: International Baptist Studies (edited). Carlisle: Paternoster, 2002.
Modern Christianity and Cultural Aspirations (coedited with Tim Larsen). London: Sheffield Academic, 2003.
The Mind of Gladstone: Religion, Homer and Politics. Oxford: Oxford University Press, 2004.
The Dominance of Evangelicalism: The Age of Spurgeon and Moody. Leicester: InterVarsity; Downers Grove: InterVarsity, 2005. Korean ed., Seoul: InterVarsity, 2012.
Protestant Nonconformist Texts: The Nineteenth Century (coedited with Kenneth Dix and Alan Ruston). Aldershot: Ashgate, 2006.

Books Published by David Bebbington

Congregational Members of Parliament in the Nineteenth Century. Cambridge: United Reformed Church History Society, 2007.

Baptists through the Centuries: A History of a Global People. Waco: Baylor University Press, 2010.

Victorian Religious Revivals: Culture and Piety in Local and Global Contexts. Oxford: Oxford University Press, 2012.

Interfaces: Baptists and Others: International Baptist Studies (coedited with Martin Sutherland). Milton Keynes: Paternoster, 2013.

Evangelicalism and Fundamentalism in the United Kingdom during the Twentieth Century (coedited with David Ceri Jones). Oxford: Oxford University Press, 2013.

The Intellectual Attainments of Evangelical Nonconformity: A Nineteenth-Century Case-Study. London: Dr. Williams's Trust, 2014.

Index

Note: Page numbers in **bold** type indicate a photograph.

A

Abelard, Peter, 48
Abington Avenue Congregational Church, Northampton, 49–50, 51
Abulafia, David, 45
Acadia University, 83–84
After Henry (DVD film), 99
Alice's Adventures in Wonderland (Carroll), 6, 32
All Saints' Scholarship, Nottingham High School, 19
Alsace-Lorraine question, 109
"Amazing Grace" (hymn), 113
American Baptist history, 94
Amos, prophet, 112–120
Ancient Times: A History of the Early World (Breasted), 28
Antiquities of Nottinghamshire (Thoroton), 32
Ashford, Daisy, 102
Atkinson family (David's father's cousins), 8
Augustine, 126

B

Baptist Historical Society (BHS), 76, 79
Baptist Historical Society Summer School, Spurgeon's College, 27
Baptist Identity course, Truett Seminary, 94
Baptist Quarterly, 76, 79
Baptist Union of Scotland, 76
Baptists in Scotland, The (Bebbington), 92
Baptists through the Centuries: A History of a Global People (Bebbington), 94
Barber, John, 43, 44
Barth, Karl, 40, 80
Battle of Flodden (1513), 10
Baylor Institute for the Study of Religion, 124
Baylor University Press, 94
Baylor University, Texas, 87–89, 94
BBC Radio, 103
Beasley-Murray, George, 42
Bebbington, Agnes, née Threlfall (paternal grandmother), 9
Bebbington, Anne (cousin), 14
Bebbington, Anne (daughter)
    adoption of, 65–66
    age 2, with David, **67**
    age 21, with David, **70**
    America travel, 82, 87, **88**
    Australia travel, 83
    birth of daughter Becky, 70
    birth of son Daniel, 70
    dyslexia, 69
    marriage to David Cumming, 70

135

Index

Bebbington, Clarice "Vera," née Urquhart (mother)
  adherence to strict routines, 4–6
  with Bill and David aged 9 months, **4**
  birth of David, 3
  Brethren Assembly influence, 13
  chiropodist training, 13
  at David and Eileen's wedding, **52**
  David's PhD graduation, 47
  death of, 11, 13, 56, 68
  engagement to Bill, 27
  heart attack, 51, 68
  home town, 3, 11–12
  meeting and marrying Bill, 9, 13
  Nottingham Women's Bible Society, 42
  schooling, 11, 12
  Scottish background, 11
  taught world is full of dangers, 8
  thirst for general knowledge, 7–8
  writing by, 11–12
Bebbington, David
  academic accomplishments, 19, 22, 39, 47, 54
  academic focus, 39
  activities, at Cambridge, 36–37
  adoption of Anne, 65–66
  age 9 months, with parents, **4**
  age 2, **5**
  age 15, with father, **31**
  age 29, as author of *Patterns in History*, **74**
  age 37, with Anne, **67**
  age 56, with Anne, **70**
  alcohol consumption, 38
  architecture interest, 29–30
  athletic endeavors, 18–19, 21
  background, 8–15
  baptism, 27
  Baylor University, 87–89, **88**
  Bible Society secretary, 42
  Biblical studies, 25
  board game collection, 32–33, 98–99
  book collection. *See* book collection and collecting
  book reading, 6, 32–33
  books published by, 28, 89–95, 133–134
  bus number collection, 33
  chapel committee elections, 41
  childhood illnesses, 7
  Chinese restaurants, 42, 101
  Christian faith activities, 40–43, 79–81
  Christian faith, commitment, 23–27
  Chronic Fatigue Syndrome/ME, 67–68, 74, 80, 82, 93
  church and civic activities, 76–78
  computers, 74–75, 101–103
  current endeavors, 97–98
  curriculum vitae, 131–132
  education, belief in, 103
  education of, 15–23, 35–39
  Eileen, engagement to, 51
  Eileen, meeting, 48
  Eileen, photo with, **100**
  essay technique, 43–44, 75–76
  family, 3–8, 47–56, 64–71
  family group in Waco, Texas, **88**
  favorite films, DVD, 99
  first book written by, 28, 89
  first car, 55
  Fitzwilliam College, 39, 54, 57, **58**
  as forensic investigator, 105
  geography interest, 32
  heraldry interest, 29–30, 98
  history, development of interest in, 27–30
  history and geography, inseparable, 105
  history course, Cambridge, 43–47
  history department, Stirling, 72–73
  history lectureship, 56
  home in Bridge of Allan, 64, **65**
  home in Cambridge, 52–55, **53**, **55**
  honeymoon, 51–52
  Hulsean Prize winner, 47
  Jesus College, 22–23
  knight collection, 27
  learning to drive a car, 55, 60
  learning to ride a bicycle, 50–51
  lecture series, 44–45
  lecturing style, 59

Index

library work, 21–22
modern technology, 101–102
on modern trends, 103
musical appreciation, 56
notes on services, 26, 40, 97–98
Nottingham High School, 19–20, **21**
PhD research, 46–47
poetry venture, 59
political interests. *See* political interests
politics, 109, 113
preaching, 58–59
research fellowship, 39, 54, 57
research students, 85–86
retirement prospects, 101–102
Robert Hall Society, 48–49
St. Deiniol's Library fellow, 94
in secondhand bookshop, **96**
Seely Primary School, 15–19, **16**, 28
sermons, 26, 58, 80, 112–120, 121–130
shorthand method, 30, 98
social skills, 23
student life, 38
teacher training, 75
teaching, 56–57
television watching, 33
travels and conferences, 81–85
trips. *See* trips and travel
UK projects, 78–79
University of Stirling, 71–76
utilitarian view of university, 103
wedding, 51–52, **52**
Bebbington, Eileen, *née* Lacey (wife)
adoption of Anne, 65–66
America travel, 82, 87, **88**
association with Gladstone, 99
Australia travel, 83
baptism, 55
Bible study leader, 99
book club at Stirling, 65–66
Christian commitment, 50
education, 48, 99
engagement to David, 51
first car, 55
Girton College attendance, 48
home in Bridge of Allan, 64, **65**
home in Cambridge, 52–55, **53**, **55**
home town, 49, 99
meeting David, 48
photo with David, **100**
Robert Hall Society, 48–49
teaching assignments, 51, 53, 65, 66
wedding, 51–52, **52**
Bebbington, Ernest (cousin of father), 14
Bebbington, Harold Leach (paternal grandfather), 8–9, 14, 24
Bebbington, Janis (aunt), 14
Bebbington, John (cousin), 14
Bebbington, John Harold (uncle), 9, 10, 14, 24
Bebbington, Madge, later Jones (aunt), 4, 9, 14, 27, 98
Bebbington, Paul (second cousin), 14
Bebbington, Penny (cousin), 14
Bebbington, Roger (cousin), 14
Bebbington, Sam (brother of grandfather), 14
Bebbington, William "Bill" Edward (father)
on atom bomb, 9
birth of David, 3
chiropodist training, 9
with David aged about 15, **31**
death of, 9
education, 9, 10
engagement to Vera, 27
lung cancer, 9, 13, 51
meeting and marrying Vera, 9
parents and siblings, 9
with Vera and David aged 9 months, **4**
World War II, 9
Bebbington family ancestry, 10, 24
Bebbington quadrilateral, viii, xv, 1, 91
bed and breakfast establishments, 60
Belvoir Castle, Leicestershire, 27
Bible, first reading of, 32
Binfield, Clyde, 86
Birmingham University, Alabama, 82
Black, Alasdair and Susan, 80
board game collection, 32–33, 98–99
Bolton, Robin and Rosemary, 59–60
bomb threat, during Northern Ireland troubles, 46

Index

book collection and collecting, xii–xiii, 33–34, 52, 61–62, 95–97, 100, 102
  See also secondhand bookshops
books published, 28, 89–95, 133–134
bookshops. *See* secondhand bookshops
Booth, William, 48
Bradlaugh, Charles, 123
Breasted, J. H., 28
Brethren Assembly
  in Aspley, 23–24
  beliefs, 23
  in Nottingham, 9, 11
Britain, European connection, 108
British and Foreign Bible Society, 42
British Library, London, 45
Broadcast Talks (Lewis radio presentation), 124
Broadmead Baptist Church, Northampton, 50, 51
Broughty Ferry Baptist Church, Scotland, 76
Brown, David, 77
Brown, Jay, 105
Buildings of England (Pevsner), 30
Bunyan, John, 127
bus number collection, 33
Butterfield, Herbert, x
Buxton, Thomas Fowell, 119

C

C. S. Lewis Society, 92
Calvin Quatercentenary Conference, Geneva, **85**
Cambridge Heraldic and Genealogical Society, 36
Cambridge University Library, 45
Cambridge years
  academic activities, 36–37
  books and book collecting, 61–62
  Christian faith activities, 40–43
  education, 35–39
  family life, 47–56
  history activities, 43–47
  Jesus College building amenities, 35–36
  political interests, 62
  preaching activities, 56–59
  teaching activities, 56–59
  trips and travel, 59–61
Cambridgeshire Baptist Association, 58
Campbell, Roy, 72
Cannadine, David, 45
Carey, William, 108
Central Baptist Association, 80
Chadwick, Owen, 78
Channon, W. G., 55
Chapman, Alister, xn8
Charge, Sidney, 51
Charity, Jocelyn and Michael, 102
Chinese restaurants, 42, 101
Chitnis, Anand, 72
Christ across the Disciplines: Past, Present, Future (Lundin), xvi, xn8
Christ Church, Oxford, Tom Quad, 78
Christian Discussion Group (CDG), 25–26
Christian historians, 76
"Christian Scholar and the Scriptures, The" (Bebbington)
  apologetics, 123–124
  communication, 124–125
  conclusion, 130
  confidence, 127–128
  delight, 128–129
  as example of David's thinking, xvi
  freedom, 126–127
  grace, 122–123
  mediation, 129–130
  obedience, 125–126
  overview, 121–122
Christian Unions (CUs), 36, 40, 80
Christianity and History (Butterfield), x
Christianity and History Forum, 76
Christie, Agatha, 33
Chronic Fatigue Syndrome/ME, 67–68, 74, 80, 82, 93
Chubb Lock and Safe Company, London, 46
Church, The (Küng), 42
Church on Its Past, The (Clarke and Methuen), xvi
Clarke, Peter D., xvi, 47

Index

Classics Faculty Library, Cambridge, 61
Coffey, John, xi, xn8
Coleridge, Samuel Taylor, 37
Collander-Brown, Frank, 20, 25
Collingwood, R. G., 102
"Come Down, O Love Divine" (hymn), 27
commentary readings, 80
computers, use of, 74–75, 101–103
Concert Manager, Nottingham High School, 22
Conference on Faith and History (1967), x
Conferences on Modern British History, 77
Congregationalism, 20, 26, 50, 51, 79, 99
conscientious objector (Alec Urquhart), 11
Cooke, Alistair, 37
Counties of England (Mee), 30
"County of Inverness, Scotland, The" (Urquhart), 11–12
Covedale Road house, Nottingham, 3, 4, 13, **14**, 68
Cowley, Ian, 34
Crawford, Michael, 45
Crimean War (1853-1856), 128
Cumming, David (son-in-law), 70
Currents in World Christianity project, 84
curriculum vitae, 131–132
Cushing, Geoffrey, 19, 20, 78

D

Dawkins, Richard, 123
D'Elia, John, 86
diphtheria, childhood illness, 7
"Discipline of History and the Perspective of Faith since 1900, The" (Bebbington), xvi, xn8
Dissenting Academies Project, 122–123
"Dissenting Idea of a University, The" (Bebbington), 47
Doddridge, Philip, 49, 113
doing things versus believing things, 26

Dominance of Evangelicalism, The (Bebbington), 94
Donation of Constantine, 109
Dr. William's Centre for Dissenting Studies, 79
Dr. William's Library, London, 79
Duffy, Eamon, xiii, 42
Duke University, North Carolina, 82
dyslexia, 69

E

East Cliff Church, Bournemouth, 49
East India Company, 114
e-books, 102
Ecclesiastical History Society (EHS), xvi, 78, 81
Ecclesiology Society, Cambridge, 36
Edstrom, Anna, 67
Elizabeth, Queen, coronation, 6
Elliott, Dick, 19–20, 29
emancipation, of slaves, 119
Emmanuel Congregational Church, Cambridge, 99
Erskine, John, 113
Eskridge, Larry, 86
essay writing, Cambridge, 43–44, 47
"Evangelical Discovery of History, The" (Bebbington), xvi
evangelical historians, xi
Evangelical Quarterly, 98
evangelicalism, viii, 113
Evangelicalism and Fundamentalism in the United Kingdom During the Twentieth Century (Bebbington and Jones), 84
Evangelicalism in Modern Britain (Bebbington), viii, xi, 91, **92**

F

Faraday, Michael, 128–129
Finley, Moses, 43
Fisher, Vivian, 44

Index

Fitzwilliam College, Cambridge, 39, 54, 57, **58**
Fletcher, Stella, 78
Flinders University, Adelaide, 83
Forbes, Duncan, 45
Ford, Henry, 107, 111
Forsyth, Jessie, 99
Forsyth, P. T., 26, 99
Fox, Celia (previously Hammond), 49
France, Anatole, 96
Franco-Prussian War (1871), 109
Free Church Women's Council, 50
Freeman, E. A., 109

G

Galloway's bookshop, Cambridge, 61
Garden House Riot, Cambridge (1970), 37
George, William, 79
Gilley, Sheridan, 42
Girton College, Cambridge, ix, 38, 48, 49
Gladstone, Sir William Erskine, 93
Gladstone, William Ewart, 44, 62, 73, 90–91
Gladstone Centenary Essays (Bebbington), 93
Gladstone diaries, 93
Gladstone family Bible, 97
Gladstone's Library, Hawarden, Wales, 93
Gladstonian Liberalism lecture, 93
Gordon College, Massachusetts, 81
Gospel in the World: International Baptist Studies, The (Bebbington), 85
Graham, Billy, 127
grammar and punctuation, 103
Great Reform Act of 1832 (Britain), 119
Great St. Mary's Church, Cambridge, 40
Gregory, Brad S., xn8

H

Hall, Robert, 61
Hammond, Celia (later Fox), 49
Hancock's Half Hour (DVD film), 99

Harrell, Ed, 82
Harrison, Paul and Audrey, 83
Hawarden Castle, 93
Hayden, Roger, 51, **52**
Heffer's bookshop, Cambridge, 61
Hegel, G.W.F., 108
Heraldic and Genealogical Society, Cambridge, 36, 37
heraldry interest, 29–30, 98
Herodotus, 109
High Anglican services, 42, 98
Historians' Study Group, Scotland, 76
"History of Ideas and the Study of Religion, The" (Bebbington), xn8
History of Political Thought, course, 43
Hofmeyr, Hoffie, 82
Holmes, Arthur, x
Holmes, Finlay, 81
Holy Trinity Church of England, Cambridge, 40
Honest to God debate (Robinson), 26
Horder, Morley, 35
Howes, John, 42
Hulsean Prize (University of Cambridge), 47
Hyson Green trip, 18

I

Idea of a Christian College, The (Holmes), x
Idea of a University, The (Newman), 125
In the Shadow of the Pulpit (Thomas), 126
India
    Christian missionaries, 114
    military occupation, 100–101
Inspector Morse (DVD film), 99
Institute for the Study of American Evangelicals, 84
intellectual historian, xi
Interfaces: Baptists and Others: International Baptist Studies (Bebbington and Sutherland), 85
International Conference on Baptist Studies (ICOBS), 83, 85
International Historical Congress, 81

Index

Inter-Varsity Fellowship, 62
InterVarsity Press, 90
interview techniques for historical research, 90
Ireland, Protestant ascendancy, 107
Israel, on settlements in West Bank, 109
Ivanhoe (Scott), 32

J

James II, King, 107
Janet and John readers, 32
Jeffrey, Ken, 73, 86
Jeffrey, Linda, 73
Jestice, Arthur, 40, 48
Jesus College, Cambridge, 22–23, 35, **36**, 79
John's gospel, distribution to Cambridge undergraduates, 42
Johnson, Samuel, 110
Jones, Alan (cousin), 4
Jones, Kevin (cousin), 14
Jones, Madge, née Bebbington (aunt), 4, 9, 14, 27, 98
Jones, Margaret (cousin), 4
Jones, Mary, 42
Jones, Michael (cousin), 14
Jones, Norman (uncle), 4, 14
Jones, Trevor (cousin), 4
Journal of Ecclesiastical History, 78

K

Kaunda, Kenneth, 40
Keiss Baptist Church, Scotland, 77, **77**
Kidd, Richard, 53–54
Kidd, Rosemary (*née* Margetson), 54
kinesiology, 67
Kitson Clark, George, 46, 57
knight collection, 27
Küng, Hans, 42

L

Lacey, Caroline (sister-in-law), 70
Lacey, David (father-in-law)
    church and civic activities, 49
    civil engineer career, 49–50
    as Congregationalist, 49
    contribution to David's PhD, 46–47
    at David and Eileen's wedding, **52**
    death of, 56, 68, 83
    later years, 68
    meeting Margaret, 49
    move to south coast, 55
    multi-infarct dementia onset, 68
    taught David to drive a car, 55
Lacey, Jonathan (nephew), 49, 71
Lacey, Katharine (niece), 49, 71
Lacey, Margaret (mother-in-law)
    church activities, 50
    coffee at David's, 49
    as Congregationalist, 49
    at David and Eileen's wedding, **52**
    death of, 56
    gave car to David and Eileen, 55
    later years, 68
    London University degree, 49
    meeting David, 49
    move to south coast, 55
    teaching career, 49–50
Lacey, Michael "Mike" (brother-in-law), 49, **52**, 70–71
Lacey, Sheila (sister-in-law), 49, **52**, 68
Larsen, Timothy, xiii, 86, 123
lecture series, Cambridge, 44–45
lecturing style, 59
Letter from America (radio broadcast), 37
Lewis, C. S., 92, 123–124
Life of Gladstone (Morley), 33
Lifeway, Bible class, 99
Lloyd George, David, 79
Lloyd-Jones, Martyn, 48
Lundin, Roger, xvi, xn8

M

Maiden, John, 86

Index

Mansfield, Nottinghamshire, 3, 4, 8, 9, 11, 12–13, 16, 17–18
Mapp and Lucia (DVD film), 99
Margetson, Rosemary (later Kidd), 54
Marsden, George, xi, 82, 127
Matthew, Colin, 93
McWhinnie, Hugh, 80
ME (myalgic encephalomyelitis). *See* Chronic Fatigue Syndrome/ME
Mee, Arthur, 30
Mellers, Dame Agnes, 19
Members of the Scottish Parliament (MSP), 78
Mere Christianity (Lewis), 124
Methodists and Methodism, 57, 102, 114, 122
Methuen, Charlotte, xvi
Milner, Isaac, 113
Milton, John, 95
mind, training of, 110–111
Mind of Gladstone: Religion, Homer, and Politics, The (Bebbington), ix, 93
modern technology, 101–102
Montefiore, Hugh, 40
Morgan, Densil, 86
Morgan, Kenneth, 47
Morris, Glyn, 24
Mulberry Harbour, 50
Munro, David, 56
music collection, 56
musical appreciation, 56
myalgic encephalomyelitis (ME). *See* Chronic Fatigue Syndrome/ME

N

Nagaland, India, 100–101
National Library of Scotland, 46, 79
National Library of Wales, 46
National Public Radio, 103
National Swimming Academy, Scotland, 71
Nazis, rise to power, 108–109
"New Being, The" (Tillich), 26
New Evangelical Historiography, xi
Newman, John Henry, 125

Newnham College, Cambridge, 47, 57
Newsome, David, 45
Newton, John, 113
Niebuhr, Reinhold, 40
Nietzsche, Friedrich Wilhelm, 102
Noll, Mark, A., xi, xn8, 84, 92, 93, 94
Nonconformist Conscience: Chapel and Politics, 1870–1914, The (Bebbington), ix, 90
Nonconformists
    basis for David's PhD topic, 49
    Cambridge subculture, xii
    Liberal Party leanings, 62
    Members of Parliament, 79
    Nottingham community, 49
Norman, Edward, 44
North Atlantic Missiology Project, 84
Northampton
    historical sites, 50
    as strong Nonconformists area, 49
Northampton High School for Girls, 50
Northern Ireland troubles, bomb threat, 46
Notre Dame University, Indiana, 82
Nottingham, history project, 28
Nottingham High School, 19–20, **21**

O

Odyssey (Homer), 17
Oklahoma Baptist University, 89
online resources, 103

P

Page, Sir Denys, 43
Parnell's Irish Party, 44
party-line telephone, 54
Patterns in History (Bebbington), x, xv, 90, 94
Payne, Ernest, 27, 76
Penguin Bookshop, Nottingham High School, 22
People of One Book, A (Larsen), 123
Perry Mason, fictional character, 111

Index

Perse School for Girls, Cambridge, 53
Perth College, Scotland, 69
Peters, David, 29
PhD research, 46–47
Phillips, Charlie, 1, 86
Pitt, William, 115
Play Manager, Nottingham High School, 22
Pocket Testament League, 24
poetry venture, 59
Poirot novels, by Agatha Christie, 33
Poirot series (DVD film), 99
"Political Dissent" lecture (Bebbington), 57
political interests
    at Cambridge, 37–38
    History of Political Thought, course, 43
    Liberal Party leanings, 62
    Nagaland military occupation, 100–101
    "Political Dissent" lecture, 57
    as political historian, ix
    in Scotland, 77–78
politics
    history and, 109
    religion and, 113
Porter's bookshop, Cambridge, 61
Postmodernism, 90
Practical View of the Prevailing Religious System of Professed Christians, A (Wilberforce), 117, 118
preaching, Cambridgeshire Baptist Association, 58–59
Protestant Nonconformist Texts (Bebbington), 94
Psalm, sermon on, 121–130
Puritans, 126–127
Pusey, E. B., 123

Q

Quakers, 127
Queen Mary University of London, 79
Queensberry Street Baptist Church, 24, 25

quotations collection, 37

R

Rad, Gerhard von, 80
Randall, Ian, 86
Rawlyk, George, xi, 82–83, 85
Regent College, Vancouver, BC, 81–82
Religion and Society Project, 84
research, for PhD, 46–47
Research Assessment Exercises, 104
research fellowship, 39, 54, 57
Rise and Progress of Religion in the Soul (Doddridge), 113
Robert Hall Society
    David and Eileen's meeting, 48–49
    David's association with, 40–43
    Eileen as president, 51
Robinson, John, 26
"Rock of Ages" (hymn), 93
Roman Catholics
    civil rights for, 115
    in Northern Ireland, 107, 108
    services, 42, 98
Rugg, Julie, 86, 96
Rutherford, Samuel, 126–127

S

Sails, Andrew, 26
Sainsbury, Lord of Turville, 111
St. Andrew's Street Baptist Church, Cambridge, 40, **41**
St. Deiniol's Library, Hawarden, 93
St. Edward's Passage, Cambridge, 61
St. Mary Magdalene Church, Oxford, 62
Sandemanians, 128
Schama, Simon, 45
Scott, Sir Walter, 32, 110
Scottish Baptist History Project (SBHP), 76–77
Scottish independence, 78
Scottish Institute of Sport, 71
secondhand bookshops, 1, 34, 50, 61, 83, 96–97, **96**, 100

Index

See also book collection and collecting
Seeing Things Their Way: Intellectual History and the Return of Religion (Chapman, Coffey, and Gregory), xn8
Seeley History Library, Cambridge, 44
Seely Primary School, Nottingham, 15–19, **16**
seminars, at Cambridge, 57
sermons, 26, 58, 80
services notebook, 26, 40, 97–98
Shaftesbury, Lord, 62
Shaftesbury Project, 62
shorthand, development and use of, 30, 98
Sidmouth, Lord, 114
Simeon, Charles, 27, 105
Skinner, Quentin, 45
slave trade, 116–119
Socrates, 102
Southern Methodist University, Dallas, 89
Spurgeon, C. H., 108
Staley lectures, 82
Stanley, Brian and Rosey, 84
Starkey, David, 39
Stephen, James, 115
Steuart, Sir James, 108
Stirling Baptist Church, 65, 77, 79–81
Stirling Castle, 71
Stirling Council of Churches, 77
Stirling University. *See* University of Stirling
Stott, John, 36, 79
Strivens, Robert, 86
student riots, Paris (1968), 36
Studies in Church History (EHS publication), 78
Sutherland, Gillian, 57
Swift, Roger, 93

T

Talbot, Brian, 76, 86
Taylor, Helen, 65
Taylor, James, 65, 79–80
teaching, at Cambridge, 56–57
See also University of Stirling
Teaching Quality Assessment team, 75
1066 and All That (Sellar and Yeatman), 102
Thatcher administration, 39
Thimann, Eric, 20
Thimann, I. C., 20
Thomas, Adam, 29–30
Thomas, Dylan, 126
Thompson, David, 46
Thompson, E. P., 38, 57
Thornton, Henry, 115, 117
Thornton, Robert, 32
Thoroton Society of Nottinghamshire, 29, 89
Through the Looking Glass (Carroll), 6, 32
Tillich, Paul, 26
Tom Quad, Christ Church, Oxford, 78
Tranter, Neil, 72
Trinitarian schema, 26
trips and travel
　America, U.S., 81–82, 83, 105
　Australia, 83
　Bath, 59–60
　bed and breakfast establishments, 60–61
　Belfast, Northern Ireland, 81
　Canada, 81–82, 83
　Fiji, 83
　map usage, 101
　New Zealand, 83
　Northampton, 50
　Nottinghamshire, 29
　with parents, 27, 30–31, **31**
　planning for, 102
　South Africa, 82, 84
　Stuttgart, Germany, 81
　summer (1969), 59
　to view great houses, 27
　West Country, 60
Truett Seminary, Texas, 87, 94
Tuck, Richard, 44
Turl Cash Bookshop, Oxford, 61

INDEX

U

Union Theological College, Belfast, 81
Unitarian Historical Society, 79
Unitarianism, 79
United Reformed Church History Society, 79
universities
  purpose of, 38–39, 103, 125
  student population change, 73
  UK government discussing cutting or closing, 73
  utilitarian purpose of, 103
  See also specific schools
Universities and Colleges Christian Fellowship, 80
University of Pretoria, 82
University of Stirling
  academic semester system, 71–72
  background, 71–72
  changing nature of, 73–74
  character of, 71
  geographic setting, 71, **72**
  history department, 72–73
  history lectureship, 56
University of Tennessee, Chattanooga, 89
University of the South Pacific, 83
Unwin Hyman publishers, 91
Urquhart, Alexander "Alec" (maternal grandfather), 11, **12**, 15
Urquhart, Clarice Evelyn, *née* Martindale (maternal grandmother), 11, 15, 32, **52**
Urquhart, Keith (cousin), 7, 14, 16
Urquhart, Nancy (aunt), 14
Urquhart, Peter (cousin), 7, 14, 16
Urquhart, Roy (uncle), 11, 14
Urquhart, Wendy (cousin), 7, 14, 16
Urquhart Castle, 11, 60
"Use of History, The" (Bebbington), xvi, 107–111

V

Victorian Nonconformity (Bebbington), 94

Victorian Religious Revivals: Culture and Piety in Local and Global Contexts (Bebbington), xi, 94

W

Wagner, 102
Waller, Gordon, 23, 26
Ward, Reg, 78, 105
Warwick University Limited (Thompson), 38
Wayper, Lesley, 57
Weimar Republic, Germany, 108
Wesley, John, 122
Wheaton College, Illinois, 81, 82, 83, 84
Wilberforce, William, 90, 112–120
William Ewart Gladstone: Faith and Politics in Victorian Britain (Bebbington), 93
William III, King, 107
"William Wilberforce and Christian Duty" (Bebbington)
  conclusion, 119–120
  courageous statement, 117–118
  defense of the weak, 116–117
  as example of David's thinking, xvi
  persistent goodness, 118–119
  public justice, 114–115
  vital religion, 112–114
Wilson, Linda, 86
Winnie the Pooh (Milne), 6, 32, 102
worship trends and styles, 98
Wragg, Mrs., 51

Y

Yeager, Jonathan, ix, 1, 86
Young Historians' Group (Cambridge), 45–46
Young Visitors, The (Ashford), 102

Z

Zion Baptist Church, Cambridge, 40, 50, 51, 53

www.ingramcontent.com/pod-product-compliance
Lightning Source LLC
Chambersburg PA
CBHW051108160426
43193CB00010B/1359